NEW HOPE FOR PLANET EARTH

Next Page: Dr. John Haggai (left) and Dr. Jack Sparks.

NEW HOPE FOR PLANET EARTH

John Haggai

Publishers since 1798

THOMAS NELSON INC.
NASHVILLE / NEW YORK

Library of Congress Cataloging in Publication Data

Haggai, John Edmund.
  New hope for planet Earth.

  1. Evangelistic work.   2. Missions. I. Title.
BV3790.H26   269'.2   73–21518

To Johnny
my Number One son, buddy, and
prayer partner
whose passion for Christian outreach
and whose patience in adversity
wonderfully reflect the heart
and mind of Christ
irradiated through Johnny's
remarkable mother

Contents

Three students at the Haggai Institute

Preface

Admittedly, planet earth is in trouble. Inflation is world-wide. Our currency is cancerous. Our Social Security system is bankrupt. The use of drugs is frightful. For example, Judge Claude Shaw of Atlanta has recently said that he estimates that fifty percent of the people in his court have had something to do with drugs. Pornography is pervasive. The pornographers have been "fighting for their rights," but they are now infringing on our rights. By the checkout girl in the grocery are magazines filled with nude and lewd pictures. The home is breaking down; there is an alarming increase in divorce. Taxes are skyrocketing; more than thirty-seven percent of America's income is going for taxes. Many other nations of the world are suffering similarly. We have plummeting church attendances. There is a pleasure-mad syndrome. Instead of using the affluence that God has given for world evangelization, people have turned Sunday into fun day and virtually eliminated the thought of God on the weekend. The West is marked by an overreliance on technology and armaments—along with prayerlessness. A similar mood of materialism grips some Eastern nations, such as Japan. Ecological imbalance and disaster prevail.

Men's hearts are failing them for fear. There are wars and rumors of wars. There is pestilence; there are physical upheavals.

Nevertheless, the explicit command of God is that we

are to occupy until Christ comes. Paul the Apostle certainly had as much to discourage him when Nero was on the throne. Yet he wrote Philippians from Rome. You read it in vain to find any nuance of discouragement. There is none whatsoever. Paul made it clear that he was "almighty in Christ, who continually keeps pouring his power in me," which I believe is the best translation of Philippians 4:13. He was confident that the Lord will supply all of our needs. He had no room for a do-nothing attitude, twirling our thumbs in desperation, talking about the impending doom and the coming of Christ.

The new emphasis on the coming of Christ is certainly proper. The Bible stresses the return of our Lord. Yet there is almost no emphasis in much of the material today on heaven, on the enthroned Lamb, on the joy of fellowship with the saints. If you read the books and listen to the messages and peruse the articles on eschatology, too often you get the impression that those who are looking for "the blessed hope" are looking for an escape from the problems that are confronting them. There is an unconscionable desire to check out before the bills are due for which there is no money to pay.

We must look for the return of the Lord as though he may come at any moment, but we must plan and work as though he may not come for a thousand years. This is the conviction that underlies this book. It is the commitment that underlies my work through Evangelism International, a program that acts to carry the gospel around the world. Enter with me, through the pages that follow, into my conviction that God is alive and powerful. He has not been defeated, and He continues to win victories throughout the world today. This is not hearsay or wishful thinking. I have seen it—on every continent.

Several years ago, I read a book that touched my mind and heart deeply. I felt that I had to communicate with the author, but locating him required three years! Since that experience, I have resolved to supply adequate identification on any book that I should write. My address is Box 13, Atlanta, Georgia, 30301. My phone is area code 404, 633-9553. If you wish to visit me at the office, you come to 2751 Buford Highway, the fifth floor of the Day Building.

There are wide-open opportunities for Christian service and witness in many parts of the world today, but these opportunities are not in the form traditionally assumed by Christians of the West. We can go to many nations of the Third World, those nations of Asia, Africa, and Latin America that are not aligned with the West or with the Communists. When we go, however, we must go as servants. Not only so, but there are many areas into which we cannot go directly at all. Missionaries from the West are strictly forbidden in much of the world. It is this challenge which is met by the program of Haggai Institute in Singapore. Here, Christian leaders from the Third World study together and share with each on how to carry the gospel to their own peoples. This unique program opens doors that otherwise are shut. Not only so, but it has the great advantage of using Christian nationals to reach their fellow countrymen. Missionaries from the West are still needed where they can go, but the gospel is needed in areas where Western missionaries cannot go. The command of Christ is to go to *all* nations. This is the order under which we must serve.

1

The Hope Is Real

There's hope for planet earth.

This is my profound conviction.

Some are seeing only signs of impending destruction, but I see signs of hope.

Ultimately, of course, our hope as Christians is for the visible, victorious return of Christ. He is coming, as He promised, with power and great glory. That truth is as certain and as central for the Christian as the Pole Star is for navigators throughout the northern hemisphere. Everything that follows in this book rests on that assurance. It gives us motive power. This lays the foundation for our hope.

Till He Comes

But what about the present? Christ may return tonight. We cannot be certain of the date in advance. The proof that we are looking for His coming is to be demonstrated by how diligently we are occupied until He comes. Christ said, "I must work the works of him that sent me, while it is day" (John 9:4). He also said, "As my Father hath sent me, even so send I you" (John 20:21).

13

Too often, Christians get into little spiritual coteries and develop into "Bless Me Clubs." They say, "Here I am; I'm a Christian. Now, Speaker, get up there and bless me." While there is blessing in studying the Word, truth that is not applied is truth denied. The tragedy is that so many have mistaken growth in knowledge for growth in grace. The accumulation of scriptural knowledge does not automatically produce conformity to Christ.

To be sure, there must be communion with Him. There must be that time of solitude where we know Him in the power of His resurrection and the fellowship of His sufferings. As we know Him, our style of living becomes more akin to His.

We must live in the awareness that Christ may come any morning or any night. Somebody asked John Wesley, "If you knew that Jesus were to come in the next twenty-four hours, what changes would you make?" He said, "Not a one." Everything that he did was postulated on the assumption that Christ might return at any moment. But how he lived! How he gave his life to declaring the glad tidings!

Horatius Bonar, nineteenth-century, Scottish leader, went to the window every morning and said, "Maybe today, Lord, maybe today." Every night, it was, "Maybe tonight, Lord, maybe tonight." But the proof of his Christian dedication lay in the fact that he was occupied in witness until Christ should come. He was not trying to figure out such things as whether the latest political developments could be identified in prophetic Scriptures.

It seems to me that there are people today who are in danger of doing what some Christians did in the 1930's. They talked obsessively about the revival of the Roman Empire. They spotlighted Mussolini as the Antichrist. As Vance Havner said, the downfall of Mussolini was not half as embarrassing to the Italian people as it was to some leading Bible teachers. Some had to buy up or burn their books. Any eschatology (doctrine of last things) that has to change with the headlines of the paper is not a biblical eschatology.

We thank God for the renewed emphasis that Jesus is coming to earth. The proof of our commitment shows through our conduct. Christ has given us the Great Commission.[1] What are we doing about it?

Our hope is for the return of Christ, but that does not mean that the present is hopeless. Some are looking only for impending destruction, but I see signs of hope for real victories for Christ here and now.

It's not that I don't know the hazards and the needs.

In more than fifteen years of leadership in evangelism, I've seen the needs. I've felt the pulse of a dying world.

But this isn't all I know.

I know the saving grace of Jesus Christ. I know the heart of the loving Father God. I know the power of the Holy Spirit to change men and even nations.

I know that the purpose of God for mankind is not destruction and damnation but redemption.

Peter put it this way more than nineteen hundred year ago: "Beloved, be not ignorant of this one thing, that one day is with the Lord as a thousand years, and a thousand years as one day. The Lord is not slack concerning his promise, as some men count slackness; but is longsuffering to us-ward, not willing that any should perish, but that all should come to repentance" (2 Pet. 3:8-9) .

[1] "Go ye therefore, and teach all nations, baptizing them in the name of the Father, and of the Son, and of the Holy Ghost: Teaching them to observe all things whatsoever I have commanded you: and, lo, I am with you alway, even unto the end of the world" (Matt. 28:19–20) .

As Peter goes on to say, we can't know in advance when God will bring the present earthly order to a close, but we do know why he is delaying: "The longsuffering of our Lord is salvation" (v. 15).

It also is clear what our response should be. "Be diligent" (v. 14); "beware lest ye, . . . being led away with error of the wicked, fall from your own steadfastness" (v. 17). Verse 18 says, "Grow in grace." If the Lord is coming immediately, why grow?

God's purpose for man, therefore, is crystal-clear.

So is his purpose for us.

We are not called to wait for him but to go for him. He is already there ahead of us, waiting for us to follow.

My personal philosophy is that we are not entitled to any opinion on any moral or spiritual question where God has spoken. We have no right to personal opinions on the Great Commission. The only adequate response is unquestioned obedience.

In order to obey, we must:

First, have knowledge of peoples, places, and conditions in foreign areas. The Commission is not just to go to our own neighborhood or even nation but to every creature.

Second, we must distribute the church's energies, prayer emphases, time, and money equitably . . . compatible with the heart of God, who loves the whole world. "God so loved the world" (John 3:16).

What loving parent would lavish 90% of the total attention, money, prayer, time and energy on only one of four children while grudgingly sharing the remaining 10% with the other three children? The little chorus sung by Sunday School children declares the truth:

"Jesus loves the little children
All the children of the world
Red and *yellow, black* and white
All are precious in His sight.
Jesus loves the children of the world."

Third, we must direct the greater attention and output to the points of greater need. The sick child commands greater attention and receives greater assistance from the parents (and brothers and sisters) than the child who enjoys robust health. One Christian worker for every 700 Americans compared to one Christian worker for every 100,000 Indians is a travesty of compassion and commitment.

Fourth, the gospel must be communicated in terms of the prospects' cultural environment. We must never change the essence of the gospel: "But though we, or an angel from heaven, preach any other gospel unto you than that which we have preached unto you, let him be accursed" (Gal. 1:8). We must adapt the *expression* of the essence. Jesus made a totally different approach to the woman of Samaria from that of Paul to the men of Athens. Nevertheless, they each shared the same gospel in both cases.

All the resources necessary to obey our Lord's Commission are available. This includes manpower, materials, and money. "Ye have not because ye ask not."

Our business is to bring Christ to men rather than to bring men to Christ. There is no one scheme by which the world will be saved, but in the main, nationals reach nationals. The New Testament and Christian history corroborate this.

How can we hope? There is only one way—men's reconciliation to God and to each other through Jesus Christ. There is no shortcut, no easy way. Governments can't bring peace. Education can't bring it. Business and industry can't bring it. Psychology and sociology can't bring it. Only Christ can bring it.

For the past nine years, my ministry has been worldwide. I've been around the world several times—not on glamor trips but on gospel treks. Major crusades have been conducted in Indonesia, Korea, Singapore, Portugal, Lebanon, India, and other scattered places. In these crusades thousands have made their professions of faith in Jesus Christ. So I see signs of revival. I see signs that men are turning to Christ. I see the practicality for carrying the good news, as Christ commanded us, "to every creature" (Mark 16:15).

Later in this book, I will be talking to you about the great needs and fantastic problems of spreading the gospel today. I'll be talking about God's purposes and his resources. I'll be talking about an updated and proven solution to the problems of an exploding world population wary of the West and, in many instances, oblivious to God. I'll be talking about a global movement some leaders credit with laying the foundations for peace. I'll be talking about the consequences we face if we fail to carry the good news. But first, let me tell you what some other Christians and I are doing now to carry out Christ's Great Commission.

Cross Roads of the East

Come with me to Singapore, the cross roads of the Orient. This great city of more than two million people is situated, incredibly, within three thousand miles of half of the world's population.

Yes, I said half. Half of the world's people are as close

to Singapore as the greatest distance across the continental United States.

To the northwest of Singapore are the masses of India. To the northeast are those of China and Japan. East and southeast are the islands of Indonesia, one of the world's most fruitful fields for Christian expansion. The Philippines are not far away, where a tribe of stone-age men completely cut off from other humans was recently discovered. New Guinea lies to the east. Here headhunters still roam the jungle.

Singapore itself is a mosaic of the world's peoples. The Chinese are the most numerous, but there also are large groups of Malays, Indians, and Europeans. Religions include Buddhism, Hinduism, and Islam, along with a Christian minority.

But the importance of Singapore is far more than geographical. For nearly a century and a half, this cosmopolitan center was a key outpost of the British Empire. For fifteen years now, it has been independent. And the record-shattering development of this republic under the superb and sterling leadership of Prime Minister Lee Kuan Yew is without precedent.

Singapore is completely neutral. Here people from all of the world's nations can meet on ground that is free of domination by either the West or the Communists. A man from any Third-World nation can come here. When he returns home, he carries no taint, no suspicion that he has been influenced by Western imperialism.

Singapore today is the strategic center for reaching mankind. In the days of the apostles, we can see that God prepared the way by providing a universal language—Greek —and the excellent roads and law and order of the Roman

Empire. Paul and other missionaries were able to go from city to city preaching the gospel. Similarly, we now can see the hand of God in preparing Singapore as the place from which to reach the world today.

For reasons to be made clear in later chapters, we can't go to many of the world's places and peoples to carry the gospel. We can instead, however, bring Christian leaders to Singapore and prepare them to go back to their homes. There they can train their own people to carry the gospel. For every age, God has his method and his people. As the world changes, God adopts effective strategies. This is what He is doing today.

An Asian from America

How did a Syrian boy from Louisville, Kentucky, reach exotic Singapore? This story starts in Damascus, the oldest inhabited city of the world. There my father grew up as a Christian in the anti-Christian atmosphere of the Turkish Empire. Brutality was the order of the day. My father and his family suffered the hostility unleashed on those who followed Christ. At the age of fifteen, he was sent by his parents—at great sacrifice and risk—to America. Here he arrived without money or family, to find a place for himself and later begin a family of his own.

This is not the place to relate all of the details. But when you consider all that my father went through to find a home here in a land of freedom and opportunity, it is no wonder that I love America.

Yes, I love America. Like my father, I have been blessed by its bounty. Yet my roots in Asia make a difference. As I have traveled over the world—especially since 1968—I have come to understand what many Americans do not see.

America is generous with its wealth. No other nation in

history has given to others on such a lavish scale. But that is not the whole story. America not only gives but it also gets from others. Americans have a way—often unintentional—of dominating places and situations where they are. They approach others on the assumption that the American way surpasses all others. In spite of all its generosity and good intentions, our nation is not deeply loved in many places around the world. In many places its wealth is resented. In many places its power is feared.

Here is where my Asian background makes a difference.

My face shows my Syrian ancestry. To the people of Asia, I look like an Asian, not a Westerner. But it's more than a matter of looks. I have an empathy for the people of Asia. I appreciate their sensitivity and their pride. Dr. W. A. Criswell, pastor of the world's largest Southern Baptist church, has said of me, "John Haggai is a natural for the work he is doing. He is a Syrian. The Arab people know and love him. He is welcome throughout the entire Eastern world."

The peoples of Asia and the rest of the world—just like us Americans—want to determine their own destinies. As we love our nation, they love theirs. As we feel pride in our way of life, they feel pride in theirs. Nor do they always see our ways as superior to theirs. To many Asians, the affluence of America is not a sign of superiority but of false values. They see us as taking too much stock in material things and not enough in spiritual ones.

It was a stinging rebuke that the Pakistani educator, Dr. M. A. Q. Daskawie, delivered in Singapore. He said it with love, but the facts were painful to those of us from the West. He referred to "the decay in morals that has come about in the wake of a permissive, affluent society. To the people in our part of the world Western nudity and drinking are far worse than what goes on nearer home. The freedom of action, thought and speech which are the hallmark of Western culture are completely misunderstood and misrepresented."

On anther occasion, an Asian, in good spirit and with no malice, told us that students in Central Asia referred to a Western coed as a "moron with less on."

The fact that our alleged commitment to Christ has not produced a distinctively Christian moral climate tends to neutralize the impact of Western Christianity in non-Christian communities.

Dr. Criswell has expressed the problem in strong words: "From what I can understand . . . the Eastern world has had its fill of Western domination. Whether it is good or bad, the Eastern world wants to be free of us, to wash their hands of us."

Here's the rub. To many people of the East, Christianity is identified as a Western religion. To many, it is a means of cultural imperialism, a way that Westerners have of trying to make Easterners over into their own mold. Again, Dr. Criswell has put it well: "Christ didn't live in our part of the world and the Christian faith didn't arise in our civilization and culture. It is theirs."

Yes, it is theirs—as well as all men's. But so many are not open to seeing that until the good news is brought to them by people of their own nationality.

Tragic? How true. Yet you can understand it when you really stop to think about it. You pay more attention to people of your own race and nation than you pay to others. How much attention do you pay to the Asian—there are some—who comes to America and tries to convert you to Buddhism or Islam? It's natural for us to respond to people like ourselves, and it's natural for everyone else, too.

A New Beginning

Phase four of a massive evangelistic program that I led in Indonesia included training Indonesians to evangelize their fellow nationals. This occurred in 1968, and from it came a new beginning in seeking to win the world. The effectiveness of training Indonesians to witness to Indonesians opened my eyes to the need for training national Christians around the world.

As the idea began to take shape, selected Christian leaders from several nations were brought to neutral Switzerland in the Fall of 1969 to be trained in practical ways of telling others about Jesus. A second program of this type was carried in Switzerland early the next year. But the need was for a location much closer to the peoples we had to reach. Thus Singapore was identified as the place to be. We began our first session there in February, 1971.

Later, I will tell in detail of the kind of training we offer, the kind of men we are training, the kind of leaders who serve on the faculty, and so forth. I will tell of results— sharing the testimonies of some who have been trained. This is a program that already is working, and the evidence of its effectiveness is massive. Let me preview this here by sharing the evaluation of one Christian leader from the third world.

Dr. Roland J. Payne is the bishop of the Lutheran Church in Liberia, West Africa. He is one of the world's distinguished black Christian leaders, holding six degrees, including two earned doctorates. He attended the second training seminar that was held in Switzerland. He writes:

"I will never forget the ministry and the witness that we encountered in Switzerland. What he [John Haggai] has started, which we know as Evangelism International, should have been started twenty years ago.

Nam Dam Crusade, Seoul, Korea

"Yes, it is true that we need missionaries. But we need nationals to study evangelism and return to their own homes to bring the Gospel of Jesus Christ to their own people. They are the best equipped witnesses.

Concerning his own training in Switzerland, Dr. Payne has said, "I was able to get something that I had never gotten before at school. With all my experience, with all my traveling, with all my degrees, I never got that practical thing . . . and I can assure you it will make the Lutheran Church a better church in Liberia and wherever my influence shall exend for the Gospel of Jesus Christ."

Act on Your Hope

1. During daily devotions direct your attention to the truths of Christ's imminent return.

2. Meditate on the command to "occupy till I come" (Luke 19:13). A right understanding of Christ's return doesn't discourage involvement in Christian witnessing; it stimulates this involvement.

3. Expand your knowledge of world conditions, opportunities, and needs. One possibility is through requesting *Straight from the Shoulder,* which carries such news with reports of the work of Evangelism International. Address the request to Box 13, Atlanta, Georgia, 30301.

2

Stop Segmenting the World

The pulse of the world beats fast and faltering. Anxiety runs rampant. Many people lack resources to cope with problems that beset them from all sides. It doesn't take a Mayo Clinic examination to identify an abnormally high pulse beat or irregular heart throb. Nor does it take a genius to conclude that the heart of the world is sick and very possibly deteriorating more rapidly than men admit. Pressure created by fear soars. Love, the life-blood of human survival, suffers critically poor circulation.

The Edge of Doom?

The chorus of the leaders of our time comes out more a dirge-song than the sound of festivity. As the Archbishop of York has said, "The writing on the wall of threatened doom and destruction can now be read clearly by all thoughtful men."

Our technology improves at a dizzying pace—but with what result? As man expands his powers, he expands his powers to do evil. "Nuclear fision suggests less the conversion of the earth into a paradise than the opening of the sixth seal of the last judgment, when there came a great earthquake; and the sun became black as sackcloth of hair, and the moon became as blood." This is the lament of Dr. Schuman in his book, *Soviet Politics at Home and Abroad.* Dr. John A. Simpson, chairman of the Executive Committee of Atomic Scientists, testified before a special Senate committee, "It seems to me at the moment that we have a very short time to put our house in order." Robert Hutchins, former chancellor of the University of Chicago, is quoted as saying that the world would destroy itself within five years.

All of these statements were made more than twenty years ago. The men who made them were not wild-eyed rumor mongers with an irresponsible mania for discussing apocalyptic destruction. They were scholars whose credentials cannot be impeached. Nearly a quarter of a century later, the planet earth and her inhabitants continue to live and move and have their being. Why?

Former British Prime Minister Clement Attlee has been quoted as asking, "Who can deny but that had Adolf Hitler the power to do so, he would have destroyed the world when he destroyed himself?" For several years, now, there have been men who have it in their power to destroy the earth. The heart of man has not changed. How, then, does one explain survival to this moment? It can be explained only in terms of the restraining power of God. Humanly speaking, one miscalculation, one human error, can trigger off a nuclear holocaust.

God has spared us through the exercise of his restraining power on the forces of evil. Dr. William Lawrence, for so many years science editor of the New York *Times,* said in 1946, "Atomic energy is here to stay. Are we?"

It is notable that the following was published in the New York *Times* without comment shortly after the first atomic explosion: "Knowing this first, that there shall come in the last days scoffers, walking after their own lusts, and saying, Where is the promise of his coming? for since the fathers fell asleep, all things continue as they were from the beginning of the creation. For this they willingly are ignorant of, that by the word of God the heavens were of old, and the earth standing out of the water and in the water: Whereby the world that then was, being overflowed with water, perished: But the heavens and the earth, which are now, by the same word are kept in store, reserved unto fire against the day of judgment and perdition of ungodly men. But, beloved, be not ignorant of this one thing, that one day is with the Lord as a thousand years, and a thousand years as one day. The Lord is not slack concerning his promise, as some men count slackness; but is longsuffering to us-ward, not willing that any should perish, but that all should come to repentance. But the day of the Lord will come as a thief in the night; in the which the heavens shall pass away with a great noise, and the elements shall melt with fervent heat, the earth also and the works that are therein shall be burned up. Seeing then that all these things shall be dissolved, what manner of persons ought ye to be in all holy conversation and godliness, looking for and hasting unto the coming of the day of God, wherein the heavens being on fire shall be dissolved, and the elements shall melt with fervent heat? Nevertheless we, according to his promise, look for new heavens and a new earth, wherein dwelleth righteousness."

These words from the Bible were written nearly two thousand years ago by the Apostle Peter under the inspiration of the Holy Spirit of God. Norman Cousins was speaking neither foolishly nor fantastically when he said that the year 1945 ought to be called 2945. In that year, when the atomic age was born, mankind leaped a thousand years. Did it leap towards destruction or did it leap towards development?

We must not miss the relevance of the word written by Peter nearly two thousand years ago. The word for "elements" is *stoicheia* in the original, which means "elemental particles by which the universe is constructed." In our everyday language we call it "atom." Peter says, "The atom shall melt with fervent heat." He further says that these elements, these *stoicheia,* these atoms, shall be dissolved. The original word for "dissolved" is the simple word *luo.* This word has in it the idea which we find in the modern splitting of the atom in nuclear fission.

It is true that Peter and his contemporaries knew nothing of the atomic nucleus, but the Spirit of God did. I am not suggesting that Peter predicted the atomic bomb, but he certainly set forth an intriguing idea in light of today's knowledge of nuclear fission. The nontheologically oriented New York *Times* felt that these words of Peter merited special attention after the detonation of the atomic bomb in Japan.

Turning the World Upside Down

Man's future is determined by his relationship to God. This relationship is dependent upon commitment to Jesus Christ. Jesus said, "I am the way, the truth, and the life: no man cometh unto the Father, but by me" (John 14:6). Christ is the *way* for sin, the *truth* for ignorance, and the *life* for death. Without Him, hearts are troubled by sorrow that has no solution.

The one fact that gives credibility to these words of Jesus Christ is His bodily resurrection from the grave after His death and burial. The New Testament gives us overwhelming evidence that the resurrection of Christ is a fact. By rising from the dead, Jesus converted his disciples from a fearful, disheartened band into the bold preachers who "turned the world upside down." Peter was moved from denial to fearless affirmation. Thomas was changed from doubt to certainty. Paul was stopped cold on the road to Damascus by the risen Christ and devoted the rest of his life to telling of his experience. He assured the Christians in Corinth that more than five hundred had seen the risen Christ at one time in Palestine. Most of these were still living when he wrote his first epistle to the church in Corinth, Greece. Human imagination cannot account for the resurrection. Fraud cannot account for it. The change in the disciples and the unanimity of their testimony can be explained by only one fact: Jesus actually and literally rose from the dead. It has well been said that the resurrection of Jesus is the best-attested fact of ancient history. It is doubted only by those who choose to ignore the evidence.

But we are concerned with more than the fact of the resurrection. The resurrection demonstrates the deity of Christ—His divine authority to command the allegiance of all men. It proves the truth of His claims for Himself and of His teachings to us. We are under His command.

Before He ascended to heaven, Jesus left instructions as to how His gospel—His "good news," His "glad tidings"— should be delivered to all men. He further declared that when man acted upon this news, he would enter into a right relationship with God and with his fellow man.

A small group of people—about 120—took Him literally. They obeyed His command. They changed the complexion of the then-known world within one generation. They did not persecute, nor did they high pressure. They never resorted to subversive means in their efforts to "make disciples" for the Lord Jesus. They simply presented Jesus Christ as a viable option—as God's answer for man's need. They relied upon prayer, the power of the Holy Spirit, the "love of God shed abroad in their hearts." Their own personal experience and witness administered a powerful influence for God among men.

Don't forget the Communists were not the first people who set out to win the world. First-century believers in Jesus Christ predated them almost two millenia. Unlike the Bolsheviks, who fought (and fight) with every available weapon, these believers used only the weapons Christ provided. They needed no iron curtain, no shelter of secrecy, no hush-hush weapon. They could openly advertise their weapons—love, prayer, power of the Holy Spirit— and the belligerents against both God and man were helpless to oppose.[1]

Christianity Today

The early Christians gave their lives—in living or in dying—to carry out the mandate of Christ to carry the gospel to every creature. Unfortunately, today's Christians are failing to carry out this mandate. Too many, while professing to know Jesus Christ in a personal way, engage in personal, social, and business practices that negate everything Jesus is and came to do.

My friend, Rev. Justin Harris, National Methodist pastor of Bombay, India, told me that he had visited recently in the city of Moscow. During his visit there he was thrilled

[1] I differentiate between Christianity as a system and the aggregate of those believers who are committed to the person of Jesus Christ. Devotees of the former have resorted to all kinds of anti-Christian activities like some of the inquisitions in the name of Jesus Christ. Those of the latter group have never inflicted punishment and persecution upon *any* peoples.

to see twelve young people baptized into the Baptist church at Moscow. He finally made contact with one of them and explained his amazement and his delight. He said, "I could understand it if you were older people, but you folks have grown up under the rule of atheism. Explain to me how it is that you gave your lives to Christ and now have followed Him in baptism." Their answer was, "The irresistible power of holiness." The lives of some of the Christians were so vibrant with the power of God these young people were impelled to seek salvation in Christ.

An outstanding European Christian businessman, who has for years carried on extensive business in all areas of the world, including mainland China and Russia, said to me that some feel the following statement could be documented. "There are more believers in the Lord Jesus Christ in Soviet Russia today than in any other nation of the world, including the United States of America." Russian leaders said to a friend of mine that they knew where every underground church was but that they were leaving them alone because every time the finger was put on any one of them, it simply multiplied. Mrs. Kosygin was known to be a faithful attendant to the services of her underground church each week until she went to heaven a short while ago.

Let's examine the situation. An overview is important. When you look at a panoramic picture, you don't hold it so close to your face that you see only one person in it. You get the full significance of the picture by looking at the whole. Unfortunately, many people fail to apply this to their view of the world. They feel that what is good for their particular area of society—as insulated as it may be—is good for everybody else. Thus they project a provincial Christ rather than the universal Christ.

For instance, the vast majority of the world's people consider Christianity a Western religion. The fact, of course, is just the opposite. Jesus was born in Asia. He exercised His entire ministry in Asia. He died in Asia. He was buried in Asia. He rose from the grave in Asia. He ascended to heaven from Asia. In spite of these truths, well-meaning but ill-advised Westerners have attached Western cultural trappings to Christ's gospel. The true meaning of the gospel has been obscured. As a result, millions languish in fear and unbelief, assuming that the gospel is for Westerners only.

What have been the results? Well, notice these facts. In 1800, there were about 200,000,000 Protestants in the world. Today, there are just slightly more than 200,000,000 Protestants. While the number of Protestants has practically stood still, the population of the world has run away. In 1800, Protestants accounted for 25 percent of the world's population. Today, they account for less than 6 percent! And the percentage keeps decreasing.

Let's look at things from a slightly different angle. Instead of directing attention to the Protestant population, let's consider the total Christian population—Catholic, Protestant, Eastern Orthodox, and all. The world's population increase is nearly 80,000,000 people a year. (Note that that's more than a third of the entire Protestant population!) The net increase for Christendom—using the word in its broadest possible sense—is about 7,000,000 a year. In other words, the world's population is increasing more than eleven times as fast as the Christian population. And that Christian increase, of course, counts all of the babies that are baptized. It is not an increase at all in terms of actual believers. In terms of the total population of the world, we are winning (counting the babies) less than 19/100 of 1 percent of the world's people.

Let's face the facts. We are not winning the world for Christ. We are losing it for Him.

Part of the problem is the one-sided distribution that we make of Christian resources and efforts. The tragic truth is that only an estimated six percent of all the world's ordained ministers and missionaries deal with more than two-thirds of the world's population. Ninty-four percent for one third, six percent for the other two thirds. How can it be? It's like trying to fix a leaking faucet while a dam is bursting. Are these God's priorities? Is this what the Holy Spirit is leading us to do? Is this carrying out Christ's Great Commission?

Do we really believe that the Lord is "not willing that any should perish"? Do we really believe that he has commissioned us to go into "all the world"? Do we understand that "all the world" is not just geography but human life? Christ is sending us to go to people where they are and as they are. The Commission is not to make them over into our image but to tell them about the crucified and risen Savior. We are to rely on the Holy Spirit. We are to give every man an opportunity to hear and say yes to Jesus Christ.

Let me correct two errors. The first is an unfounded and unscriptural assumption that people everywhere are searching for Christ and want a personal relationship to Him. The Bible denies this. God's Word says, "There is none that seeketh after God" (Rom. 3:11). It further says that "Men loved darkness rather than light, because their deeds were evil" (John 3:19). Even since Adam, man in his sin has been hiding from God. The Bible makes it quite clear that no man comes to God except he be drawn by the Holy Spirit. No one can truly confess Christ as Savior except by the gift of the Spirit.

Yes, men want God's approval. They look for peace. They crave freedom from fear. They revel in religious pomp and ritual, creeds and other trappings that give them a sense of winning God's favor. But none "seeketh after God." In other words, they want God on their own terms, not on His. They are seeking a god of their own liking— one they can manipulate—not the living God who stands above man's sinful desire.

Therefore, those who know the truth must declare it. Men are truly lost. They are so thoroughly lost that they do not even know they are lost. "How shall they believe in him of whom they have not heard?" (Rom. 10:14). We cannot blithely assume that the world's billions can find their way without hearing the good news.

The second error that must be corrected is that through a sophisticated "marketing" procedure, we can persuade men to accept Christ. We certainly ought to use all of our technological sophistication—communication capabilities, transportation availabilities, computer hardware, and other modern means to communicate the good news. But our confidence must rest solely upon the Holy Spirit to vitalize the message and quicken the reponse in the human spirit.

We must remember that part of Christ's Commission is, "Lo, I am with you." We are go under His leadership— guided and empowered by Him, relying on His presence, seeking His will.

In my world ministry, I refuse to employ any kind of psychological pressure to "push" a person towards a commitment to Jesus Christ. My whole objective is simply to present the "good news." The effort is not to make converts but to give every man an opportunity to hear the gospel. It is not our responsibility how men respond to the message. That is God's work. It is our responsibility, under His leadership, to take the message to them.

How tragic! News of the death of Joseph Stalin girdled the globe in two minutes. The death and resurrection of Jesus Christ are still unknown to multiplied millions the world around.

I assert again the fact of new hope for planet earth. This hope arises out of a faith that, by de-Westernizing the gospel and internationalizing Jesus, our generation can observe a new and unprecedented ministry of gospel witness to all nations among all peoples.

Act on Your Hope

1. Learn about persons living in your community from nations of the Third World, such as Latin America, Africa, or the Orient. One possible source of information is a college or university, where students from Third-World nations may attend. Consider the possibility of making the acquaintance of one or more such people, perhaps by an invitation to dinner in your home; use this as an opportunity to learn about the person's nation—its customs, its occupations, its religions, and so forth.

2. As you read the Bible, look for indications that God is concerned for people of all racial and national backgrounds. Slip a sheet of paper into your Bible on which you copy verses (and where they are found) that show, as Peter put it, that "God is no respecter of persons" (Acts 10:34).

3

Act—Don't React

It is a tragic fact of experience and history that we tend to be correction-prone rather than prevention-prone. In other words, we wait until the tragedy hits before we act. We tend to react rather than to act. We repair better than we build. We analyze the past better than we plan for the future.

Dr. F. Olen Hunt, distinguished retired Methodist minister, served his denomination for many years in the areas of stewardship and missions. This sainted man, now well into his eighties, told me of hearing a striking statement by Dr. John R. Mott in 1905. Mott said, "Give me a thousand missionaries for Japan or within fifty years we'll send 200,-000 of our boys with guns and bayonets."

We didn't send a thousand. We gave Dr. Mott six missionaries for Japan. And Dr. Mott's prophecy was wrong. It wasn't fifty years; it was thirty-six years. It wasn't 200,000 of our boys; it was 1,000,000 of our boys. It wasn't guns and bayonets; it was the atomic bomb!

Had we sent the thousand missionaries Dr. Mott requested, the total costs—everything—would have amounted to less than $34 million from 1905 to 1941. But we refused. The American debt resulting from her involvement with the Japanese in World War II exceeded $90 billion before the end of 1944.

Did we learn our lesson? Apparently not.

General MacArthur, on board the USS *Missouri* in September, 1945, assured us that there must be a "recrudescence of the spirit if we are to save the flesh." He opened the way for American organizations to send 10,000 missionaries to the Orient. Once again, we failed. Who knows how the history of the Orient might have been rewritten if we had sent the gospel when the opportunity knocked on our doors.

Until Vietnam became front-page copy, there was hardly a Baptist missionary, a Presbyterian missionary, a Methodist missionary, a Lutheran missionary, an Assembly of God missionary, or a missionary from any other of the eleven major denominations there. Thank God for the Christian and Missionary Alliance. This small group had sent missionaries who did a noble work against insurmountable odds.

Had we sent the gospel to Indochina forty or fifty years ago, what would have been the result? Would we have gotten into the most unpopular war in our history? Would more than 45,000 of our boys have died there? Would more than $160 billion have been buried in that war-ravaged land?

Gadgets or Gospel?

During the 30's, 40's, and 50's we Americans tried to impress the Chinese with the number of bathtubs, automobiles, and gimmicks we enjoyed. They understood us to say to them that if they too would embrace the Christian

religion they could drive gold Cadillacs and live in luxuri-
ous homes. Though absurd and unbiblical, this conclusion
logically followed from our behavior. The Oriental mind
was much more concerned with an ideal than with things.
We seemed to equate "things" with God's special blessings. They rejected the materialism we appeared to adore.

It is true that many Western missionaries bravely and
with great personal sacrifice poured their lives into China.
And yet, in consideration of our capabilities and of China's
unequaled population, the efforts in toto were puny.

The opportunity confronts us once again—an opportunity previously undreamed of. What are we going to do
about it? True, we cannot approach the situation as we did
thirty-five years ago. People of the non-West consider the
imposition of Western structures and Western formats
nothing better than cultural colonialism and ideological
imperialism. They want none of it. If we go, however, as
"your servants for Jesus' sake" (2 Cor. 4:5) even as Paul
went to the Corinthians, the opportunities for service put
into eclipse the greatest opportunities of the past.

With our communications capability, with our transportation capability, we need not repeat the spiritual fiascos
of the earlier part of this century. We must go not to West-
ernize but to tell of Jesus. We must understand the people.
We must speak to them in terms of who they are and what
they are.

Here is an example.

One man, Dr. John Sung from Hinghwa, in a period of
fifteen years made a greater impact for Christ across Southeast Asia than scores of Christians have made in most areas
in any equivalent time throughout Christian history. He
seized the opportunity. He used what he had and started
where he was. No sacrifice did he consider too great. He

turned down lucrative offers from some of the major oil companies in America as well as some of the outstanding universities of America and the Orient.

In Indonesia alone he left a legacy of 5,000 evangelistic teams with three to a team. These young men literally changed the complexion of that delightful land. His ministry laid the base for much of the evangelical witness now in Singapore and parts of Malaysia. Likewise, his influence can be seen in Indochina and mainland China. The lives of many of Indonesia's most ardent patriots were mightily influenced by the ministry of John Sung.

John Sung earned a Ph.D. at Ohio State University. Following this, he became a graduate student in theology. During the time of theological study he became spiritually cold. He considered prayer subjective and questioned the efficacy of the blood of Jesus Christ. One night Sung went to a gospel meeting at the First Baptist Church in New York City, at the corner of Seventy-ninth and Broadway. In response to the invitation he committed his life without reservation to the Lord. He became so "turned on" for Christ that three well-meaning but misled theological leaders had him confined to a mental institution. During his 193-day confinement he read the Bible through from cover to cover forty-one times! After release he returned to China to begin his ministry of evangelism. From this time on, he wore the simple clothing of a Chinese peasant farmer.

Anticommunism with Promise

Vance Havner has said, "The average Christian is so subnormal that when a normal Christian comes along he is considered abnormal." In a similar vein, Robert G. Lee has said, "The trouble today is we are so precise we're puny."

Are we going to ignore the opportunities of this hour with a repetition of evermove fearsome and proliferating tragedies? The answer to the Communist menace is not a better national policy. It is Jesus Christ. I loathe Communism. It strikes at the heart of everything I hold dear, especially the existence of God and the supernaturalness of His only begotten Son, Jesus Christ. I must confess, however, that I know of no anti-Communist organization that has slowed Communism in its tracks. I do know of instances where the enthronement of the Lord Jesus Christ in the lives of Communist leaders has completely changed their lives and communities.

During one of our Total Evangelism—Plus projects in 1969 the key Communist leader of the capital city of a nation that shall remain nameless committed his life to Christ. His conversion brought unbelievably positive results to the city.

If all the effort and money being poured into anti-Communist projects were invested in the propagation of the gospel, the stated objects of these anti-Communist organizations would be much more rapidly implemented.

One of today's tragedies lies in an overcooperative tolerance that compromises too often on important issues. The person of Jesus Christ can never be compromised! I do not expect my Jewish friends to get irritated with me when I suggest that the Lord Jesus Christ is the only hope for the individual as well as for society. I don't expect them to get irritated with me any more than I get irritated wtih them when they ask me to buy some bonds for Israel.

A Closing World

More than half of the world is now closed to traditional missions. I thank God for the traditional Western mission approach. I'm a second generation product of Western missions. However, times have changed. A new method must be found by which the direct command of the Lord Jesus, the Great Commission, shall be obeyed. No strategy is adequate that does not take into account the inaccessibility of a vast percentage of the world's population to the traditional Western approach. Traditionally, we have relied on Western personnel, Western methods, Western formats, and Western materials. These no longer meet contemporary challenges in world evangelization.

It's a new day, with a subtle shift in the world mood. Colonialism is dead. Where Third-World nationals equate today's white, Western missionaries with yesterday's colonialism, a new approach is required.

The very name "foreign missions" gives the clue to the basic problem in many Third-World areas. There was a day when there was no alternative. The West—essentially Great Britain and America—had the message and the means. Noble pioneers: Judson . . . Livingstone . . . Salisbury . . . Paton . . . Taylor . . . braved the oceans and the jungles to take the gospel where it had never gone before.

But we are living in a different day!

There was a day when international travel was only by steamship, when communications were by mail, or the experimental telegraph, when the Bible was largely an English-language book.

Today jet planes span the globe in hours. Communication satellites link continents by instantaneous television and telephone. Hundreds of countries now have the Scriptures in their own languages.

National Christians no longer sit passively waiting for their Western brothers to bring them the Word of God. They have the gospel. They have embraced the directive of the Great Commission. They know the "why" of evangelism. They ask only to be shown "how."

This is today's need and challenge—to train these National Christians in the "how" of evangelism, and let them win their own people, in their own language, in their own customs, for Jesus Christ.

Our training center, Haggai Institute in Singapore, isn't a "foreign mission" program, operated by foreigners, using foreign methods. It is, simply, the twentieth-century means for fulfilling the first century command of Jesus Christ. It is, in the opinion of many leaders, "an idea whose time has come."

Jesus didn't say, "Go into all the world—except where you are impeded by the Bamboo Curtain or the Iron Curtain, or conflicting ideologies." There was no ambiguity or equivocation. He meant what He said. Failure to go into all the world spells disobedience to the Great Commission and insubordination to the Great Commissioner. There is a way by which the Commission can be carried out, but it will require death to self. It will demand the kind of sanctified creativity only the Holy Spirit can author.

Let's close the barn door before any more horses of opportunity get away from us.

Too Much Cost?

It never ceases to amaze me how distorted our thinking can become. Through a greedy self-protectionist attitude we hurt ourselves. It is still true and many biblical truths would undergird the statement, "Help thy brother's ship across and lo thine own has come ashore." In helping others we glorify God and also operate in our own best interest. And there is nothing wrong with self-interest. Truly, a man ought not to "think more highly of himself than he ought to think." But, every promise in the Word of God is postulated on the assumption of self-interest.

Several year ago during a crusade in Waterloo, Iowa, I appeared on a television interview program. The interviewer, who made no secret of his hostility towards the gospel, hurled angry charges against evangelistic crusades.

In one outburst he said, "Did you see how much the forthcoming Los Angeles evangelistic crusade will cost?" I told him I had not. He fairly yelled, "Five hundred and thirty-two thousand dollars."

I said, "Is that all?"

He said, "My Lord, man, what do you mean, 'Is that all?' Have you no sense of value?"

I said, "The Dr. Bernard Finch and Carol Tregoff court cases have cost the City of Los Angeles an alleged five hundred and twenty-six thousand dollars. If this forthcoming crusade does nothing but forestall just one such repetition, it will be one of the greatest investments of money the people of Los Angeles have ever made."

I was in a New England state for an evangelistic thrust several years ago. A very fine businessman and a good friend said to me, "Frankly, John, I think that there must be a less expensive way of carrying on Christian work. It's just too expensive. And you fellows talk too much about money. I'm referring to all of you—pastors, missionaries, evangelists, presidents of Christian colleges—all of you. I feel that you men just don't have good business sense and don't realize the value of the dollar."

I sat there attentively until he got through. Then I said, "Isn't it true that your son has just committed his life to Christ?"

- "Yes."

I said, "I know you're happy about that."

"Yes."

I said, "Do you not credit this present evangelistic emphasis as the means God used to bring him to salvation?"

He again replied in the affirmative.

I then said, calling him by name, "I don't like to hit you this hard, but for your own good and in the interest of God's work I must. Isn't it true that you went to see a certain young woman a few months ago? Isn't it true that you put $10 thousand in cash in her pocketbook in order to try to compensate in a small way for the fact that her unborn child was fathered by this son who has just committed his life to Christ?"

He said, "How did you know that?"

I said, "Is it true or isn't it?"

"Yes, it is true."

I then said, 'Do you believe that your son, now committed to the Lord Jesus would do the same thing?"

"No, I know he wouldn't."

I then queried, "Wouldn't it have been wonderful then if this entire set of experiences during this crusade had taken place two years ago?"

He got the point. It isn't the preachers, evangelists, missionaries, and heads of Christian colleges who don't understand the value of a dollar. It is people like this well-meaning but terribly deluded businessman, who really loved the Lord but who never properly assessed true value.

When I came home from an Asian nation a few years ago, a lady impatiently asked me why I was wasting my time in that nation. "After all," she pointed out, "the total population is only thirteen million."

I told her that I was glad she didn't determine the work of the Lord in other countries. If so, she might have denied entrance to the missionary who went to Syria and became an instrument for bringing my father's family to Christ. After all, the population of Syria was only five million!

Paul Harvey, in his dramatic fashion, has highlighted the world situation today:

"Remember Genghis Khan was a nothin', a rude, crude nomad who came riding out of the Gobi Desert with a bunch of wild riders—and conquered most of the known world.

"He had been a herder of beasts, nothing more, yet he out-generalled the armies of three empires.

"So if only in our own enlightened self-interest, we'd better get the Gospel to the barbarians before they get to us."

The values of carrying the gospel to the world are well illustrated in my own family's recent history. My brother Ted, a scientist of some note, received the L. A. Hyland Patent Award in March, 1971. He was credited with having greatly assisted in Defense Communications around the world. Two months later, my brother Tom became the youngest man in history to receive the Silver Buffalo Award which stated, "You have been called 'a messenger for God in the market place' and 'an advocate of a stronger America through rededication of spiritual resources.' " Recipients of this, the Boy Scouts' highest honor, include Bernard Baruch, Douglas MacArthur, Dwight Eisenhower, and others of that caliber.

As I reflected upon my younger brothers' achievements, I thought to myself, "Surely they cannot take all the credit. Much of the credit goes to our heritage, a godly mother and dad."

Then I reasoned further, "Dad would not have known Christ had it not been for his uncle in Damascus, Syria, who witnessed to him. The uncle, businessman turned Presby-

Right: Rev. Waddy A. Haggai, father of Dr. John Haggai

Left: Dr. Haggai and Paul Harvey

terian preacher, would never have known Christ but for a Syrian national colporteur who shared the Scriptures. The colporteur would have never known Christ had it not been for the American Presbyterian missionaries. The missionaries never could have sailed to Syria had it not been for the sacrificial gifts of the anonymous Presbyterian laymen who made it all possible."

Consider the social and survival benefits to our nation represented by the citations concerning my two brothers. On the basis of these contributions alone, the love, ministry, and money of those Presbyterian Christians of long ago have paid off incalculably.

Act on Your Hope

1. Consider what you are helping to do through your church and other channels to send the gospel to peoples around the world. Identify two or three things that you can do to make this more effective.

2. Set dates for carrying out the actions which you identify. Make specific plans as necessary, asking for God's leadership and strength. Commit yourself, under God, to completing these actions.

4

And Still They Die, Martyrs

General Eisenhower said during World War II, "There are no victories at bargain prices." This is a great truth and one that every Christian ought to absorb until it becomes part of his very philosophy.

I think it was Dr. Elton Trueblood who talked about "the cult of the comfortable." For several years now, there has been a frightening decline in the number of young people committing themselves to full-time Christian service. I am firmly persuaded that the reason is because the challenge has been removed from the message. I believe in the local church—in the primacy of the local church. After all other organizations have become nothing more than a memory, the churches will still stand.

It more than passing strange, however, that some organizations God has raised up are experiencing remarkable victories. One of the unique characteristics is that they promise young people a challenge demanding their best.

Commitment and Suffering

There is no such thing as a committed Christian life without suffering. In fact, there's no such thing as any life without suffering. The difference is that in Christian suffering God is being honored and ultimate triumphs are being forged. In non-Christian suffering, despair is the result.

Jesus said, "Blessed are ye, when men shall revile you, and persecute you, and shall say all manner of evil against you falsely, for my sake" (Matt. 5:11).

In Philippians 1:29, Paul the Apostle said, "For unto you it is given in the behalf of Christ, not only to believe on him, but also to suffer for his sake." He said to Timothy, "Yea, and all tha will live godly in Christ Jesus shall suffer persecution" (2 Tim. 3:12).

There is no way by which anyone can interpret these verses so as to eliminate the Christian's suffering for Christ.

There have been more martyrs during this century alone than during all the previous centuries of Christian history.

Suffering can be psychological as well as physical in nature. Actually, is not psychological suffering infinitely more devastating than physical suffering? Are there not people who would glady put an arm into the fire and let it burn off if doing so would eradicate the memory of a horrible deed committed earlier in life?

Suffering today may be ostracism. It may be criticism. It may be cruel indifference.

I had a friend in Florida, now with the Lord, who was by conviction a teetotaler. He would not use, sell, or serve alcoholic beverages. On a large government contract, though he was the low bidder, his bid was rejected. He had been warned that he would be expected to provide liquor for a gala affair in Washington if he expected favorable consideration. He declined. He lost the business. It nearly put him into bankruptcy.

I'm not here discussing the merits or demerits of alcoholic beverage. This man did what he did because of his commitment to Christ and what he honestly felt was the explicit teaching of the Word of God. For it he suffered. Some of his children were deprived of the quality of education he had dreamed for them. He suffered psychological as well as physical breakdown from overwork in trying to hold things together. In short, he suffered for Christ in the twentieth century.

Modern Martyrs

When the great Sadhu Sunder Singh of India committed his life to Christ, he was cast out of his home, disinherited by his father, and subjected to merciless treatment. He never harmed a hair on anyone's head. He simply spread the news of the saving love and grace of the Lord Jesus. When? In the Dark Ages? No, during the early part of the twentieth century.

You may remember the wanton murder a few years ago of Paul Carlson, a missionary to Africa. While we know about him and other Americans, most do not know of the persecution and death suffered by national believers in distant lands around the world. Who can conceive the suffering, the bloodshed, the murder, the unspeakable carnage that have taken their toll among the people of God in China, North Korea, Russia—and even in the United States.

> A noble army, men and boys
>   The matron and the maid,
> Around the Savior's throne rejoice,
>   In robes of light arrayed:
> They climbed the steep ascent of heaven
>   Through peril, toil, and pain;
> O God, to us may grace be given
>   To follow in their train!

Reginald Heber, author of these words, died in India as a missionary bishop.

Who can assess the pain and suffering experienced by Dietrich Bonhoeffer and Martin Niemoeller in Germany, by the saints of God in the Philippines, Japan, and the islands of the sea during the forties?

Dr. Kyung Chik Han, pastor emeritus of the world's largest Presbyterian church, the Young Nak Church of Seoul, Korea, has literally hazarded his life for the Lord Jesus. Three times he has been left homeless and penniless —without any possessions except the clothes on his back and the materials in his briefcase. He founded the Young Nak Church in 1945. Then the Korean conflict came in the early fifties. He and his congregation were forced to flee Seoul and move south. Towards the end of the conflict one of the elders of the church was murdered by the North Koreans just before they were pushed back north of the thirty-eighth parallel.

But it is still true, "Out of the press of suffering cometh the soul's best wine." Today this church, with its more than twelve thousand in attendance each Sunday morning, sponsors a world ministry.

I have been from one end of the Indonesian Archipelago to the other. I have seen graves the Communists dug for the Christian leaders they planned to exterminate. Thanks be to God the attempted coup in 1965 was aborted. Even so, Christians suffered martyrdom before order was restored under the superb leadership of President Suharto.

How broadminded should a Christian be? Some American Christians lead me to wonder.

The contrast with some Christian leaders of the Orient is striking. Take, for example, Dr. Cho Choon Park. He

is now pastor of the Young Nak Presbyterian Church in Seoul, the successor of Dr. Han. One day, Dr. Park and I were discussing the importance of being centered in Christ and relating all the issues of life to His will. In the course of conversation I said, "I have been interested that a man from Korea got a master's degree in theology at the same school, at the same time, and under tha same professors as a friend of mine in America. Here's what baffles me. You, the Korean, are committed to the biblical teachings of Christ. You believe in Christ's substitutionary atonement for our sins and His bodily resurrection for our justification. You believe that Jesus Christ is uniquely divine as no other man ever has been or will be. On the other hand, my American friend doesn't believe a thing, and he attributes his unbelief to the enlightenment he received during his studies."

Dr. Park responded, "Dr. Haggai, we Korean Christians are accustomed to adversity and nonacceptance. We know what it is to be rejected and denied acceptance by what young Americans call the 'in' crowd. I sometimes get the feeling that some of my American friends are more interested in being accepted by their professors and the so-called 'in' group than they are in knowing the truth and

Acting upon it." What an indictment! Yet he spoke with moving compassion.

Many today are so broadminded they have become flat-headed and they arrogate to their unbelief a superior scholarship.

No Bitterness

There is one nation that imposes the penalty of death on any citizen who professes faith in Jesus Christ as Lord and Savior. The believer is attached to the front end of a cannon and blown to bits. It must be said in all fairness that the people of this nation are among the most gentle and loving I have ever met. The penalty of death for Christian converts is the sincere expression of a religious conviction —the conviction that Christian believers are a pernicious menace to the people and to the nation.

The interesting thing I have noticed in various areas of the world is that those who really endure suffering for Christ's sake display no signs of bitterness or recrimination or attempted retaliation.

Let me state, parenthetically, that the reason I do not name the places where believers are suffering is self-evident. It is in the best interest of the Lord's work. To identify such areas would only excite unnecessary belligerence.

In one nation recently the sons and the wife of a dear pastor were beheaded. The pastor miraculously escaped. When some young men of another religion found out who had committed the heinous crime, they caught the murderers and beheaded them. They brought the heads of the murderers to the pastor and said, "We have avenged you. Here are the heads of the men who murdered your family."

The pastor replied, "Men, you cannot do this. The Lord

says, 'Vengeance is mine; I will repay.' " With such passion and love did he explain the forgiveness of his heart that he won to faith in Christ the men who had avenged him.

Those who really suffer for Christ can say with Paul, "Being reviled, we bless; being persecuted, we suffer it; being defamed, we intreat."

The Result of Discipleship

I am persuaded that the measure of satanic persecution is in direct proportion to the magnitude of spiritual power.

On a recent trip around the world I observed once again that true discipleship involves and even necessitates suffering hardship. True discipleships have always suffered, and this shall continue to be. The servant is no greater than his Lord.

James, the brother of John, was brought to the tribunal seat to be tried because of his faith. There he was martyred.

Thomas, so well known as the doubting disciple, was slain by a dart while preaching in a city in India.

Simon, brother of Jude, bishop of Jerusalem, was crucified for his belief in Christ.

Bartholomew, because of preaching to the Indians, was beaten down with stakes, then cruicified. After this his skin from head to foot was bruised and flayed. Finally, he was beheaded.

Except for John, who was banished to the Isle of Patmos, not one of the twelve disciples died a natural death. All were martyred.

My observations at home and around the world convince me that it is folly for anyone to think he is a fine Christian and faithful follower merely because he is enjoying the comforts and joys of the world. The true disciple suffers today even as he did nineteen hundred years ago, but there is joy even in suffering. "We ought to obey God rather than men" (Acts 5:29).

Pliny the Younger said concerning Christians who were being murdered in Rome during the first century, "These Christians don't mind to die. They sing while they are being burned alive at the stake because they believe in one Jesus who rose from the dead."

It is important for the joy of the believer that the slanders and persecutions with which he is assailed be without solid foundation as far as his actions and life are concerned. There are some who suffer because of presumptious sins, foolhardy actions not directed by the Spirit of God, or stupid bungling. Perhaps there is no major city in America today without at least one Christian worker who has put a blight on the things of God by actions that are not only spiritually wrong but socially offensive.

It is the misery of the guilty conscience that cuts the nerve of victorious power. The man who knows he can look into the eye of God, though recognizing his own personal unworthiness and sin, knows that God sees his sincerity of heart and honesty of purpose. This man can meet the world with a tranquil mind because his conscience is clear.

There are three major reasons why the world hates and persecutes the Christian for Christ's sake.

First, the more there is of Christ in the believer, the more his life condemns the world. There is nothing that ungodly men so abhor as the unsullied purity of godly living—when it highlights the corruptness of their own hearts and lives. Jesus Christ is to the ungodly what the sun at noontide is to the diseased eye, what the bounding joyousness of the child is to the weakened nerve.

Second, the more there is of Christ in the believer, the more he offends the pride of certain ones around him. There are those who covet the admiration of true godliness which they are unable to win because of their refusal to pay the price for it. Jealousy of those who have won it is the natural result. Such envy produces hostily. Weak and carnal Christians are even led amuck.

Third, the Christ spirit in the believer is always aggressive. It compels him to attack the vested interests of wrong-doing. The Lord Jesus never expected his disciples to exert a negative influence but to preach a positive gospel. This gospel, like salt in a cut, stings when it comes in contact with that spirit that nailed Christ to the cross.

No man is to look for persecution. Christ did not come to earth in order to force men to put Him to death. He came to redeem mankind. Yet he did not shirk persecution and the cross. These were on the way towards the fulfillment of his redemptive purpose. He set his face steadfastly to the glorious end in view.

The word translated "blessed" in the Beatitudes should be translated "happy." We thus should understand Matthew 5:11—"Happy are ye, when men shall revile you, and persecute you, and shall say all manner of evil against you falsely, for my sake." This word for "happy" is the one used to express congratulations.

Don't believe that the one who is in search for the pleasures of this world and the riches of temporal things under the Christian name will find happiness in them. It is said of the soul of the church by the prophet, "All the beauty of the king's daughter is within" (Ps. 45:13). External revilings, persecutions, disparagements are promised. From these there is great reward in heaven which is felt in the heart of those who endure. Such faithful believers can say with Paul, "We glory in tribulations also: knowing that tribulation worketh patience; and patience, experience; and experience, hope; and hope maketh not ashamed; because the love of God is shed abroad in our hearth by the Holy Ghost which is given unto us" (Rom. 5:3-5).

One of the Scottish martyrs said as they were putting the fagots at his feet, "Methinks they are casting roses before me." Another said, as he died, "I was glad when they said unto me, let us go into the house of the Lord."

Acts 14, as you will remember, tells of the stoning of Paul at Lystra. The people, thinking him to be dead, left him outside the city. As soon as he recovered, he went back into the city to preach again. What a blessing he must have received—in spite of the awful ordeal. He went back for more.

It is said of the great Argyle that, as he laid his head upon the block, the physician could feel not fluttering but the quiet, steady heartbeat of health and peace. Inwardly, Argyle was sensing the happiness and receiving the blessing reserved for those who suffer for Christ's sake.

Many years ago, J. R. Miller said, "The time will never come when the way of righteousness will be the easy, flower-strewn way. Always it will be over sharp stones and amid thorns. But ever beyond the pain and the cost is the shining reward for all who will faint not in their trials."

One of the most dramatic demonstrations of this is the life and work of Watchman Nee. He has languished in a mainland China prison for years because of his faith in Christ. If you have not read his books, read them. His writings will serve as one of the greatest commentaries on this chapter you can find anywhere in this century.

Onward, Christian soldiers,
Marching as to war,

> With the cross of Jesus
> Going on before!

Unfortunately, instead of marching to war, we are limping the Broadways and the Rialtos of the world in the tight shoes of image-conscious egomania.

Nevertheless, the line is drawn. As never before, true believers can be found the world around—serving their day and generation by the will of God. Korea and Indonesia continue to experience revivals and awakenings unprecedented in Christian history. The Christians there give evidence of new hope for planet earth.

Act on Your Hope

1. Pray for those Christians who are suffering today throughout the world for their faith. Pray also for those who are persecuting them. Study and meditate on Matthew 5:44, "Love your enemies, bless them that curse you, do good to them that hate you, and pray for them which despitefully use you, and persecute you."

2. Meditate on Matthew 5:11, "Blessed are ye, when men shall revile you, and persecute you, and shall say all manner of evil against you falsely, for my sake." Is your witness for Christ clear enough that it sometimes provokes hostility? If not, face for yourself the question of whether or not you allow the Holy Spirit to fill and use you as fully as He would.

5

No Nation Is an Island

Suppose that I were a concert pianist. Suppose that I thrilled audiences everywhere after having studied in the great music centers abroad. Let's suppose that my mind possesses all knowledge of music. I come to a given city and walk out on the stage. I poise at the keyboard. Now, suppose that each finger has a brain of its own. Suppose that one says, "I'll play a note below what is written." Another may say, "I'll play blacks for whites and vice versa." Suppose a third one says, "I'll sharp the flats and flat the sharps." Another may think, "While the others are playing Tchaikovsky, I'm going to run up and down the scale."

In the meanwhile, the thumb keeps chanting, "I'm getting tired of these fingers hogging the show. I'm going to go down into the lower register and play a little ditty all to myself! I won't cooperate!"

What discord!

All Are Related

My little parable of the uncooperating fingers is an illustration of the way peoples of the world act in relation to each other.

The tragedy lies in man's insistence on self-assertion at

any cost. There is an interdependence among the members of the human body. Likewise, there is an interdependence among the members of God's created family—His world family.

Speaking geographically, of course, it is true that some nations are islands. No nation, however, is an island in the sense that it can function alone in complete disregard of other nations.

As this is being written, many Americans are wanting a scarce brand of radial tires. They cannot get them because of the war in Cambodia. Cambodian rubber is scarce. As a result, people half way around the world are being affected in this minor way.

We are now up against the fact that America does not produce enough oil to fulfill its own requirements. The situation promises to get serious within the next few years. The energy shortages beginning 1973 may be only a preview. Even with secondary recovery there is simply not the oil reserve adequate for America's needs. America then will not be self-sufficient and independent in the area of oil. Most of the known oil reserve is controlled in the Arab world. Many Arab nations, such as Libya (which has nationalized its oil), are unhappy with the United States. They consider the United States to be pro-Jewish and anti-Arab.

The situation in the Mideast today portrays strikingly the necessity for nations to understand their interdependence. It pictures the ultimate destruction of nations refusing to cooperate with others.

There has been much talk in recent years about a pipeline from Alaska. If the pipeline should be in operation by 1980, bringing a full 2.5 million barrels of oil a day to the lower forty-eight states, the United States would still be forced to import seven million barrels of oil a day from the Mideast and Africa.

A hearty breakfast illustrates the point of our inter-dependence. There is coffee from South America or tea from the Far East. Sugar may come from Indonesia, India, or Hawaii. Bananas represent Central or South America. As you eat, you listen to stereophonic recordings played on a machine imported from Japan. You are eating on a table-cloth of Irish linen, out of plates produced in Europe. Your home is heated by oil that may have come from a Mid-eastern country, transported here in a Greek or Norwegian tanker.

A woman came to me and scolded me for spending so much time overseas. As she put it, "Conditions here in America demand your ministry and concern exclusively within out continental limits." She accused me of dere-liction in my responsibilities, saying, "We can't make our nation strong when we spend all of our energies on other nations. Let them take care of themselves."

I asked her if it were not true that the bulk of her wealth was in IBM stock.

"What has that got to do with our discussion?" she re-plied.

I told her that I had just read that IBM did one third of its business overeas and that 43 percent of its profits derived from that overseas business. Even at the level of practical self-interest, we must be concerned for other na-tions. But as Christians, of course, we are called to more than enlightened self-interest.

I am constantly appalled by the lack of concern among American Christians. For instance, I find from audiences I confront that not one percent of the people in such

Christian gatherings pray systematically and faithfully for the people of mainland China. I am appalled by the attitudes that we take towards other people. People of "proper" backgrounds and good education in the West readily refer to peoples of the non-West, nonwhite nations with patronizing condescension, or worse, contemptuous indifference.

We can scarcely afford to be complacent. America's position, vis-à-vis the rest of the world, is steadily declining. James Reston pointed out in a recent column, for example, that our share of the world's gross national product has dropped from 50 percent to 30 percent since 1950. Similar declines are evident in other economic indicators. Our share of the world's monetary reserves has dropped in the same period from 50 percent to a shocking 8 percent. Japan alone now has 15 percent!

Of course, we Westerners don't have a monopoly on restricted vision. I am also appalled that some Christian groups in Third-World nations boast of sending misionaries to other nations when in reality their missionaries are sent only to their own people—their own expatriates—in those other nations.

Must war be the only time when nations form firm alliances?

I am not calling for the surrender of individual sovereignty. It is my conviction that free, sovereign nations serve their own best interests when they use their freedom to serve the total family of nations.

Unfortunately, it is usually a handful of individuals within any given nation who demonstrates compassion, concern, and awareness of interdependence. Nations should show such characteristics corporately as definitely as individuals should.

God Loves All the World

"God so loved the world." Not part but all. He did not segment the world. How can a child of God profess to love God while demonstrating contempt, or at best, gross indifference, to the peoples of the world? Such attitudes repudiate the teachings of Scripture and misrepresent the heart of God.

Francis Xavier, after 400 years, still administers the most stinging rebuke to Christian apathy and indifference. This brilliant young cavalier came to know Christ through the witness of Ignatius Loyola. Xavier was 36 at the time. The text that Loyola used was, "But what shall it profit a man if he gain the whole world and lose his own soul?"

After his commitment to the person of Jesus Christ, Xavier grieved over the nations that sat in darkness, ignorant of the light that he had discovered. Not a moment must be lost. Thousands dropping daily into Christless graves alarmed and terrified him. He set out at once. There were no comfortable motor cars, fast trains, or jet airplanes.

Xavier tramped the world till his limbs were swollen and his nerves were numb. He visited India, picking up the languages as he played with little children along the way. One day he stood amidst the sparkling splendor of an Oriental palace. Another day he paid court to a rajah and his entourage. On a third day he moved among the filthy huts of the fisher folk on the Malabar Coast.

Every day and everywhere he shared with agony and tears the strange and wondrous truth of a loving Christ whose heart embraced the whole world.

Ridiculed, stoned, and persecuted, he pressed tirelessly on, always uplifting the cross with his right hand while ringing the bell calling people to listen with his left. He made converts, planted churches, and changed the complexion of great areas of the world.

Xavier labored twenty-one hours out of twenty-four. In the course of one short decade, he learned and preached in twenty different languages before he died.

I have seen the imprint of his feet and the influence of his witness on the Malabar Coast and all the way down into Southeast Asia.

Christopher Columbus had just added a new hemisphere to the map. But, Francis Xavier enlarged the population of heaven by multitudes. He snatched people for Christ from bedouin tents, Indian palaces, Malabar fishing huts, overcrowded troop ships, robbers' lairs, pirate decks, and slaves' hovels.

With our communications capabilities and transportation facilities today, what excuse have we in our failure to go to the ends of the earth? The nearest approximation that I personally have witnessed to Xavier's type of commitment takes place today in Asia and the South Pacific.

It is understandable that men, divorced from God by sin, fail to recognize the inevitable interdependence of nations; it is unthinkable that those naming the name of Christ allow encroaching secularism and materialism to dull their sensitivities to world need.

My travel has renewed my conviction that the problem is sin in the human heart. And Christ is the only Savior from sin. The answer is regenerated men. Changed hearts! Is anything as important as introducing men to Christ? Is it as important that we pursue science and perfect economics? We can abolish disease, erase the national debt, educate everyone, and still fail to solve the problem. Men will still cheat and steal, rape and murder.

Is the answer a socialistic order upon the earth? You can

redistribute wealth and divide all land evenly among all peoples so that everyone has home, food, clothing, and necessities for physical life. The problem will remain. Inequities will return.

The problem is not Communism! If all the Communists laid down their arms tonight, we would still have the problem. Sin is the problem, and the answer is Jesus Christ.

A Canadian farmer's little boy left the house and walked out into the tossing field of wheat ready for harvest. He did not return, and his parents became alarmed. The father asked his neighbors and friends to help find the lost child. He told them to take care not to trample down the wheat. The men went, each his separate way. In the meantime an icy gale swept in swiftly off the Yukon. Hours passed, and the thermometer dropped rapidly. Ice settled down. The father became agitated about the thinly-clad child.

Finally, he drew the searching party together and said, "Men, forget about the wheat. Let's join hands and tramp this wheat down and find the boy. We'll cover every inch of ground." After a few minutes of searching a man cried out, "Here he is!" They gathered about the white, stiffened body of the little lad. He had frozen to death. The grieved father looked at his neighbors and said, "Gentlemen, we should have joined hands sooner."

I speak to every responsible citizen of the world. I speak especially to everyone who claims a personal relationship with Jesus Christ. There is no time to lose. The lost are dying, and the world is headed for chaos, apart from divine intervention. Let us join hands! Let us walk together after lost men.

Let American Christians recognize their opportunities and responsibilities to pray, give, send, and go. Let Christians of other nations, West and non-West, also pray, give, send, and go.

Later on in this book I will share some specific ways in which people committed to the will of God and the Commission of Christ can act. We must implement the Great Commission—the command of Christ to proclaim the gospel in all areas of the world.

Act on Your Hope

1. Select a nation of the world as the object of your special study and concern. Consider choosing a Third-World nation or perhaps one of the Iron Curtain countries. Read books about the nation and its people. If possible, become acquainted with a native of it who lives in your community. Learn about the religious life of the people as well as about their economics and politics. Pray daily for the spiritual needs of the people of this nation.

2. Learn about the Christian witness in this nation. Find out what Christian groups are represented, the nature of their worship and witness. Learn the names of believers. Pray specifically for these believers by name. Pray in the hope that God will effectively use their witness to win the people of the nation to faith in Jesus Christ.

6

You See Better from the Top

The place is Singapore. The year is 1970. I am standing with my friend, George Milne, on the top floor looking at the bustling streets below. George, who is a Hyatt House executive, is extolling with justifiable pride the superiority of the Hyatt House there—the largest hotel in Singapore. I am listening attentively when a sudden, random thought smashes its way onto the arena of my attention. *From the skyscraping top of that magnificent building, I cannot distinguish the skin color of the people on the streets!* Red, yelow, black, and white all look the same. In fact, I can't distinguish their relative size. A child of less than five feet looks about the same as a man over six feet.

The truth hits me with a breathtaking force. From heaven all the peoples of the earth look the same. God "hath" made of one blood all nations of men for to dwell on all the face of the earth" (Acts 17:26). We, because of inordinate egos and sin-producing fear, erect dividers and even barricades. This is cruel and totally foreign to the will of God. I do not say this academically. Nor do I base this statement only on Scripture. I speak from experience.

In 1945, my wife and I looked for a light housekeeping

apartment in Greenville, South Carolina, so I could continue studies at Furman University. Greenville is one of the most charming cities anywhere in the world. Nevertheless, people will be people. When I responded to one ad with a knock at the door, the landlady asked me what I wanted. I told her I was responding to the ad. She said, "What's your nationality?"

I chuckled. "Syrian." My father was born in Damascus, but my mother was born in this country of British ancestry. Her maternal forebears go back to the famed James Robinson of Maine who equipped, with his own funds, the Revolutionary soldiers from his area, while her paternal forebears go back to Plymouth, England. However, the map on my face was not the map of Boston or London. It was the map of Damascus. That's why I said, "Syrian."

The landlady replied, "We don't like 'furiners' here."

I told her that I was very sorry, and I asked her what her name was. She enunciated a name that was obviously French. Her husband was from France! In her thinking he was not a foreigner!

In my travels around the world I have never seen any group of people on any level that did not look down their noses at some other group of people. Arabs and Jews. Koreans and Japanese. Malaysians and Philippinos. Singaporeans and Indonesians. Irish and English.

From the top all men look the same. We know that all blood is the same. There is overwhelming evidence that responses to basic stimuli are the same. Self-preservation. Power. Love. Property. Fear. Hatred. Desire for freedom. The list is endless.

How paradoxical this world in which we live. It can produce an Adolph Hitler and an Albert Schweitzer, a George Washington Carver and a Father Divine, the NAACP and the Ku Klux Klan, an Al Capone and a Tom Dooley.

Yet, despite our diversities, our basic needs are common. And, basic to all our needs is a personal relationship with Jesus Christ, through whom we have access to God.

"Western" Gospel

John Calvin correctly asserted that of all the fields of knowledge, the two most important are the knowledge of God and the knowledge of man. Unfortunately, the pattern in the West has been to export the gospel within a Western cultural framework, ignoring the knowledge of man. Too often, well-meaning Westerners have done damage by total insensitivity to cultural mores of the non-West. In many areas, resentment is not directed to the person of Jesus Christ but to Western domination. Many non-Western people consider the approach of traditional missionaries to be nothing short of cultural colonialism and ideological imperialism.

Visiting other nations has made me keenly aware of irreparable damage done by dedicated and well-meaning people who have failed to "do their homework."

No business worthy of the name would attempt today to merchandise goods or services without adequate market research. Possibly because of a shortage of funds, or maybe just because of thoughtlessness, Christian organizations have been derelict in "researching the market." They have failed to identify and understand the peoples they are seeking to reach.

Years of experience are not necessarily the answer. Fifteen years spent in a given country do not necessarily add up to fifteen years' experience. "Practice makes perfect," but lousy practice makes perfectly lousy.

The West has too often functioned much like the fledgling student of a foreign language. He considers what he wants to say in English and then tries to translate it into the foreign language. One who is proficient in a foreign language begins to think in that language. Too often the West has laid out its objective, formulated its plan, and then, to its own undoing, attempted to impose this Western format on Easterners.

The Easterner's resentment often eludes the Westerner's observation. For one reason, people in Asia, for instance, are unspeakably polite. They would never do anything to cause another to lose face. So, the Westerner returns, thoroughly convinced that his message has been "bought" simply because there was a smile and apparent acquiescence. He does not realize that behind this smile there may be disdain by the man who says to himself, "Such effrontery! How dare he come with the arrogant step of a know-it-all from a country not yet 200 years old and try to teach basic truths to people with a 5,000-year-old culture."

Paul the Apostle was never guilty of this travesty. He never imposed the structures, the organizational format, the cultural mores of one area upon another area. He never indigenized the *essence* of Christ's gospel, but he always indigenized the *expression* of that essence.

Brash Presumption

In Indonesia several years ago one of America's respected Christian leaders went with me to visit a large and dynamic church. My American friend presumed to suggest to the pastor of the church ways in which he could improve his effectiveness for the Lord. He suggested Sunday School at 9:30 followed by morning worship at 11:00, a training period at 6:00 followed by evening worship at 7:30. He also suggested a Wednesday night prayer meeting at 7:30

preceded by a meeting for Sunday School officers and teachers. And on he went. I said nothing, but I was "dying" inside.

The Indonesian pastor politely listened to every word, responding with positive head nods and smiles. Had he been a typical Oriental, he would have said, "Thank you so much. It was so gracious of you to come here and share these wonderful ideas with me." However, behind a facade of gratitude, he would have questioned the brash presumption of the foreigner unloading his fatuous and gratuitous suggestions.

Since my Indonesian friend had been to the United States for five years of postgraduate work, he understood the American mentality. He looked my American friend in the face as he smilingly asked the simple question, "Why?"

That rocked my American friend back on his heels. Before he had a chance to answer, the Indonesian pastor graciously said, "We have a service at 6:00 Sunday morning for saints. We have one at 9:00 for sinners. You Americans try to feed sheep and convert goats at the same time. Impossible. We have separate services. In between, we have Sunday School at 7:30 which draws both groups— those attending the 6:00 o'clock service and those the 9:00 o'clock one. Do you have something better than that?"

My friend was tongue-tied. The Indonesian brother continued, "What time do your people in America get up on a Sunday morning?"

We countered with, "About 8:30 or 9:00 o'clock." (I must confess the way some look when they get to the 11:00 o'clock service is evidence they were nestled in the arms of Morpheus until well past 10:00.)

He said, "Our people get up between 4:00 and 4:30.

Furthermore, it gets very hot here, and we don't have air conditioning." He went on with the rationale for their church format. He was sweet, gentle, and considerate.

When we left, the American friend said to me, "I don't think that was a very wise thing I did in suggesting he adopt our Western procedure and structure." I assured him that this evaluation indicated that he had learned a valuable lesson which the majority of Westerners unfortunately never seem to learn.

No Carte Blanche

Seen from above, all men are the same. They have the same basic needs. The gospel of our Lord Jesus Christ meets those basic needs. We do not alter the gospel. We do alter the means of communication. The approach of the Lord Jesus to the woman by the well (John 4) was different from the approach of Paul to the men of Athens (Acts 17). The gospel was the same. The approach was different.

It's high time that we Americans abandon the self-delusion that producing the largest percentage of the world's goods and services gives us carte blanche to dominate the world's thinking. We are not rightly free to lecture the rest of the world—overtly or covertly, by direct statement or implied innuendo—on the superiority of our cultural mores. No wonder that people of the non-West think Christianity is a Western religion.

At a recent Executive Committee meeting of the Baptist World Alliance in Washington, the Chinese representative from Hong Kong said, "More of the same is not the answer." Reread that sentence. Emblazon it in your heart and mind.

We can suffer and bleed and die from a sincere desire to communicate the gospel. If we have done so in total disregard of the individual's cultural background and personal experience, the suffering and martyrdom will go for naught—accomplishing nothing positive.

Paul was all things to all men that he might save some.

There are no people on the face of God's earth who are more generous, outgoing, and loving than the Americans. However, because of our wealth, power, and extroverted natures, this compassion and willingness to help are misread in the non-West as arrogance and even churlishness.

God help us to correct our perspective so that we can be His instruments in reaching basic needs in a manner compatible with, and acceptable to, the given culture.

The answer is neither in spiritual isolation nor in Western-style hard sell. Listen to Paul: "We preach not ourselves, but Christ Jesus the Lord; and ourselves your servants for Jesus' sake" (2 Cor. 4:5). This should be the expression of our witness and service.

We are ambassadors, and we must accurately represent the kingdom in which we hold citizenship. We must represent it in both method and manner.

Remember that more than 50 percent of the world's people are yellow—and the other half are not all white!

An ambassador adheres to the laws, customs, and habits of the country he represents. He so lives and functions in the foreign country as to create the best possible response for his homeland. He does not attempt to create friction. Nor does he by lack of knowledge fail to observe the amenities so important to the people of the foreign country. "Our citizenship is in heaven." As we sit together with Christ "in heavenly places," our perspective will be as His. The indwelling Christ, filled with grace and truth, will through us communicate His grace and truth. The crucified Christ enthroned in the crucified believer still produces a magnetic power drawing all men. "There is neither Greek nor Jew, circumcision nor uncircumcision, Barbarian, Scythian, bond nor free: but Christ is all, and in all" (Col. 3:11).

There is neither Greek nor Jew—no racial barrier. There is neither Barbarian nor Scythian—no national barrier. There is neither circumcision nor uncircumcision—no ceremonial or ritualistic barrier. There is neither bond nor free—no social barrier. Let's stop routing Christ through western Europe and the United States. Let's abandon the folly of dressing Him in Western clothes, imputing to Him a Western life-style, implying to the world His message was born in the West. Let's take Him directly from Jerusalem to the point of action. Better still, let's bring Him directly from heaven to the area of human need.

And in this will lie new hope for planet earth.

Act on Your Hope

1. Examine your own attitudes about people of differing skin colors. Remember that God is the Creator; the fact that skin colors differ is part of His deliberate plan for mankind. If God loves people of all colors, what should your attitude be as a Christian? Consider not only your own attitude but whether or not your should seek to influence the attitudes of your friends and those with whom you work.

2. Examine the way in which you serve Christ as His ambassador. Consider your home, your job, your friends, the strangers you meet. In what ways are your representing Christ? Are you doing what you should, in the way you should? Remember Paul's statement, "We are ambassadors for Christ" (2 Cor. 5:20).

7

Examine Your World View

All you are—everything you think, say, and do—is conditioned by your world view. This is true no matter what your ethnic background, religious persuasion, heredity, or environment.

Every person has a world view. He has one, whether he is aware of it or not. Ultimately, all world views can be reduced to two—those that put God in the center and those that put man in the center. The view that puts God in the center can be called *theocentric,* and the one that puts man at the center, *anthropocentric.* In the theocentric view, man is moved by the conviction that it is in God that "we live and move and have our being." The anthropocentric view is well summarized in the lines, "I am the master of my fate: / I am the captain of my soul."

It would seem natural for those who put man at the center to have the greater concern for man. Paradoxically, this isn't so. Those who put God at the center embrace a social consciousness, demonstrate social concern—and do something about it.

Devotees of the anthropocentric world view have inadequate criteria by which to assess the total needs of man.

They fail to recognize man's need for God. Because they do not understand all of man's needs, they are deficient in helping to meet his needs.

It can be argued, of course, that many Christians have shown no social concern. As Christians, we should not try to avoid such painful facts. We must recognize that the professing Christian who lacks concern for human well-being has rejected the lordship of Christ. Such a person calls Him "Lord" but fails to do the things that He said.

Advent of Concern

William Wilberforce had little concern about the slave trade until he entered into a personal relationship with Jesus Christ. It was then that he played such an important role in bringing about legislation making slave trading illegal. In addition, as a result of his conversion, he compassionately dispersed his immense fortune. He did so much for the alleviation of human suffering that in his latter years he had very little of this world's goods to meet his own needs.

After William Booth entered into a personal relationship with Jesus Christ, he became obsessed with the desire to meet the total needs of the total man. What organization, what group of people, has done more in an equal period of time than the Salvation Army, which he founded? It relieves suffering and provides for man's needs, temporal as well as spiritual.

In every part of the world, I have seen the results of commitment to the theocentric view. Humble believers totally committed to the Lord Jesus Christ have erected more hospitals, founded more schools, established more orphanages, provided more humanitarian assistance than all the devotees of the anthropocentric world view put together. Go with me in imagination around the world. You will find the evidence of what I am talking about, for example, in Japan, Korea, Hong Kong, Indonesia, Singapore, India, the Mideast—all the way around the globe.

The marvelous work being done by Rochunga Podaite and his colleagues in India gladdens my heart. It began several years ago when Dr. Bob Pierce, founder of World Vision, visited India. He gave Rochunga Podaite—a young man he had never met until one morning at breakfast in a humble Indian home—money for desperately neded surgery. The doctors said that had the surgery been postponed another twenty-four hours, Rochunga Podaite would have been dead. The humanitarian concern issued from Bob Pierce's commitment to Christ.

Rochunga Podaite has come up with a new procedure for distributing the Word of God throughout the world. His organization is called Bibles for the World. He gets the name and address of everyone that is listed in the telephone directory and then sends a Bible to that person. Already the response surpasses the most optimistic expectations. People from the peasants of Bangladesh to the Jains of India to workers in Iron Curtain countries have reportedly written letters of gratitude. They also have made requests for further knowledge to help them understand the Word of God.

The outstanding center of learning in Beirut is the American University Beirut. This great school was founded by a compassionate Christian, Mr. Bliss.

One of the great hospitals of the world is the Presbyterian Hospital in Taegu, Korea, headed by Dr. and Mrs. Howard Moffatt. There are more than a quarter of a million out-patients, and more than a hundred physicians on the staff. The concern that created this hospital had its foundation in a theocentric world view.

God is absolute—absolute holiness, absolute truth, absolute righteousness, absolute love. The man with a theocentric world view has a fixed star to steer by. Man with an anthropocentric world view, on the other hand, is capricious. He is subject to faulty observations, imperfect understanding, and damaging conclusions. Consequently, devotees of the man-centered view fail miserably in the implementation of their own announced objectives.

The anthropocentric world view has sponsored humanism, liberalism, syncretism, and universalism. It says, in effect, that no religion as is as good as any religion because all men are headed for the same final destiny anyhow. (In the atheistic form, all men are annihilated at death. In the syncretistic religious form, all ultimately reach some form of salvation. The net result is the same; man is at the center in both views.)

By misrepresenting the fact that man is a creature, humanism destroys the sense of adoration for God. Man becomes his own self-contained universe—a microcosm. Humanism ridicules the importance of receiving Jesus Christ as Savior. It inflates man's imagined capability. It says there is no reason to trust God, since man can solve all his own problems. With the absence of faith in God, obviously there is no passion for evangelization. Humanism is probably the strongest deterrent to evangelism in contemporary American society. Unfortunately, I see the inroads humanism is making in many of the "Westernized" segments of the Eastern nations.

Liberalism denies any absolute truth in Christianity. It rejects biblical authority. It questions, in some instances, the historicity of Jesus. Adopting the liberal concept of the relativity of Christian truth and life means the loss of a passion for evangelization. There is, in this view, no necessity to believe in Christ.

Syncretism holds that one religion is as good as another. It scoffs at the unique superiority and deity of the person of Jesus Christ. Christian faith is unalterably opposed to it. The early church was uncompromising in its stand against Judaism and other religious and philosophical views of the time. Paul the Apostle never diluted his message so as to accommodate it to the speculations of the Stoics, Epicureans, or other intellectual systems.

Guilt Consciousness

Dr. J. S. Rhee of Korea has said, "Modern Christianity, particularly in the West, seems to have a sort of guilt consciousness in regard to other religions because Christianity under colonialism joined the white exploiters in conquering other countries and suppressing other religions. We may fully understand such psychological awkwardness toward other religions, but this is more than a psychological problem. We cannot and must not equate Christian truths with other religious teachings. If our guilt-conscious friends cannot stand firm against the danger of religious syncretism which is infiltrating Christian minds so rapidly in recent years, we Christians from non-Christian countries, that is, non-white Christians, should take over the battle."

Syncretism torpedoes any passion for evangelization because it robs the distinctive of the Christian religion. It robs the distinctive of Christ's supernaturalness. At the same time it robs all other religions of their unique beliefs and characteristics.

Universalism also torpedoes the passion for evangelization. The universalist believes that even without the communication of the gospel, every person in the world ultimately will be saved. He emphasizes the universal compassion of God—a truth taught in the Bible—but rejects the equally strong biblical truth that man must believe on the Lord Jesus Christ in order to be saved.

One need not go far to witness the throbbing growth of churches whose world view is theocentric—or the sterility of those whose world view is anthropocentric. One of the main-line denominations in the United States dispatched a survey team to determine the reasons for the expansion of their most rapidly growing churches. Each of the churches they included in the study is headed by a pastor and leadership who embrace the theocentric world view.

That same denomination could well study member churches in Japan and in Korea. In Korea, the churches are growing. In Japan, they languish. When I asked the Korean leaders about this, they told me that they felt it is simple. In Korea, the pulpit is committed to biblical theology. In Japan, it is fettered by a liberal philosophy and an anthropocentric world view. Ironically, the churches in Korea have done much more for the humanitarian assistance of their people than have their sister churches in Japan.

Historically, the people who talk only of social action have done far less for society than those who are committed to a theocentric—or specifically, Christocentric—world view.

"Dynamite"

I realize that the preceding words are dynamite. Some will take strong exception to them. But what are the facts? The evidence supports my view. I am convinced of it on the basis of looking at human life and experience around the world. In countless nations, I have seen the truth demonstrated. A man who is truly committed to Christ has an obsession to help his fellow man—not only with his spiritual needs but with his social needs.

Leckey, the classic secular historian of the eighteenth century, said, "Wesley saved England from the horrors of a French revolution." The Right Honorable Augustine Birrell, noted scholar and legislator said, "No single figure [Wesley] influenced so many minds, no single voice touched so many hearts. No other man did such a life's-work for England."

George Whitefield was the instrument of God in bringing renewal to thousands of people. During his ministry in the South he courageously published an address to the planters on behalf of the oppressed slaves. One of the most powerful figures in the anti-slavery movement in America was Theodore Dwight Weld, one of Charles G. Finney's converts. Wesley founded the first free medical dispensary in England; the year was 1746. The introduction of the Y.M.C.A. in American cities was an outgrowth of the revival of 1857. This same revival gave to society the Christian and Sanitary Commissions.

William Warren Sweet, an authority on America's religious history wrote: "The many reformed movements which swept over the English speaking world in the latter eighteenth and nineteenth centuries owed much of their impetus to revivalism. The new humanitarian impulse which lay back of all such movements has direct relationship to the revivalist's emphasis upon the inestimable worth of each individual soul." [1]

Out of the evangelical movement initiated by Wesley and Whitefield came the prison reforms in Europe instituted by John Howard, the China Inland Mission founded by J. Hudson Taylor, the mission work of John Barnado

[1] Sweet, William W., *Revivalism in America,* p. 152, C. Scribners' Sons, 1944.

in London which resulted in rescuing 70,000 waifs and the Salvation Army organized by William Booth. Leading evangelists have always been in touch with real life—"grass roots" life. They have neevr been "ivory tower brain trusters."

We hear a lot of talk about "the Christian ethic" needed today. All revivals have been ethical revivals. When a man gets right with God he is able to experience a right relationship with his fellow man. Any effort to correct man's relationship with man apart from a vital relationship with Jesus Christ is but applying the poultice of a godless self-deception to a morally- and spiritually-cancerous condition. The last half-century with its two major wars should have proved that.

The League of Nations and the United Nations with their abortive efforts are among the various humanistic measures which have failed. The so-called "social gospel" has proved a sociological flop. The sterility of education alone is quite clear from the fact that the two major Axis powers of World War II had a higher percentage of literacy than the United States.

The churches which have made the greatest impact upon society during this century have been those that have preached "the good news" of Christ's redemptive work. True Christianity recognizes that personal salvation through the gospel with its reconstruction of life is the greatest factor in bringing about genuine social improvement.

It was John Morley, the noted British author, who gave the following significant testimony: "We all have been upon the wrong track," he complained to his fellow reformers, "and the result is that the whole of us have less to show for our work than one man, Booth, of the Salvation

Army. Herbert Spencer, Matthew Arnold, Frederick Harrison and the rest of us who have spent our lives in endeavoring to dispel superstition and to bring on a new era have to admit that Booth has made more direct effect upon this generation than all of us put together." General Booth made personal regeneration basic; social reform followed. His work was wholly Christ-centered and biblical—the proclamation of the message of evangelism.

Intellectualism alone has never produced renewal. Forty-seven percent of Hitler's S. S. troops had post-graduate degrees. Those who presided over the infamy of Dachau, Auschwitz, Buchenwald and other camps of horror were highly-trained men, academically. They enjoyed the music of Bach, Beethoven and Wagner.

On the other hand, renewal has consistently stimulated intellectual development. Of the nine colonial colleges, the six established between 1740 and 1769—Pennsylvania, Princeton, Columbia, Rutgers, Brown and Dartmouth—had some relationship, either directly or indirectly, to the Great Awakening.

Princeton was the outgrowth of the evangelism of the Tennents. George Whitefield was more than casually responsible for the University of Pennsylvania and Dartmouth. Charles G. Finney was a prime mover in the growth of Oberlin in Ohio. As James Burns says in *Revivals—their Laws and Leaders,* "The immediate consequence of the reformation, therefore was to immensely quicken the intellectual side of man's nature."

Social betterment is the result of genuine renewal, not the cause. In dealing with the Ethiopian eunuch Philip did not discuss the race problem. In counseling with the Philippian jailer Paul did not discuss prison reforms. But reform followed, as Acts 16:33 makes clear.

Those who cry for a new Pentecost while rejecting the biblical message need to observe that the primary factor throughout the book of Acts—from Pentecost on—was the individual commitment of life of men and women to Christ.

Eras of renewal have always been accompanied by a revised emphasis in preaching. Preaching today has been replaced by fireside chats, without the fire. The very meaning of the word evangelism entails the idea of preaching, of proclamation. Evangelism is good news. When the heart is hot the lips cannot be cold. One cannot say convincingly what he does not feel deeply. He cannot feel deeply what he doesn't believe intensely.

Evangelism is imperative if we are to have renewal.

During recent decades, there has been a great deal of talk about union. The inference seems to be that union will bring about renewal and spiritual strength. I am persuaded that there is a mistaken confusion between union and unity. Union is fine when it is union between parties of similar nature and purpose. A union between parties of disparate nature and conflicting purpose only intensifies disunity. There can never be a profitable union of believers with unbelievers in the implementation of an alleged spiritual project. "What communion hath light with darkness?"

Tolerance is one thing. Compromise is another.

I have no time for the fractious, cantankerous, wanton splitting apart of God's people that has been perpetrated around the world in the name of "defending the faith." The body of Christ in Korea, in Hong Kong, and in the Mideast only now is recovering from the divisive attacks of an American clergyman. He recklessly assassinated the characters of godly men. He dogmatically asserted that those

groups not affiliated with his own organization were enemies of the cross. He accused them of rejecting the faith
once and for all delivered to the saints.

Unity does not require union. In Indonesia I had the
joy of directing a Total Evangelism—Plus project. It was
the first time in the history of that great land that both
Presbyterians and Pentecostals cooperated in a common
evangelistic thrust. The Presbyterians were all members
of the National Council of Indonesia. The Pentecostal
groups, with two exceptions, did not belong to the National
Council of Indonesia. Other groups also cooperated. There
was great fellowship across denominational lines between
both ministers and laymen.

Having given a great deal of time and study to this important subject, I felt led to speak on it in Tokyo, Japan.
There, Dr. Don Hoke, founder and former president of
Japan Christian College, had brought together leaders of
the major evangelical denominations working in Japan. I
based my remarks on Paul's words in Ephesians 4:1-3: "I
therefore, the prisoner of the Lord, beseech you that ye
walk worthy of the vocation wherewith ye are called, with
all lowliness and meekness, with longsuffering, forbearing
one another in love; endeavouring to keep the unity of the
Spirit in the bond of peace."

It's easy for Christians to say simply, "Christ is the answer." There is a sense in which this is true, but there also
is a sense in which it is not. Let me illustrate. Twenty years
ago I had severe trouble with my throat. The throat specialist that I consulted told me that I had an infection. He
said that it was bringing excess blood to the vocal cords,
causing swelling and obstructing the function of the cords
when I spoke. His mandate was that I must cease all speaking for two years.

Under those conditions, I did what any self-respecting public speaker would do—I went to another doctor! Strangely enough, he told me exactly the same thing. Since their prescriptions did not accommodate themselves to my desires and objectives, I disregarded both. However, the condition worsened. It appeared that my oral ministry would be short-lived.

One Sunday morning after I preached in Texarkana, Texas, a young physician, William Shields, walked up to me and said, "You've been having trouble with your voice this morning."

"Yes."

"How long has this condition prevailed?"

I told him that it had been bothering me for about ten years. He asked me if I had ever taken Teldrin Spansules. I told him that I had never heard of them and was sure that I had not taken them.

I said, "Doctor, the trouble with those medicines is that they put one to sleep. It's bad enough for an audience to get sleepy. When the minister gets sleepy, there's real trouble ahead."

He said, "I think if you'll take a spansule in the morning and one at night, you'll have no problem with drowsiness."

I did, and he was right. Teldrin Spansules were the answer to my problem.

Now here's the point. Smith, Kline, and French had been producing Teldrin Spansules for some time. They were the answer to my problem, but I had not known it. Until I knew it, Teldrin Spansules were of no more help to me than if they had never existed.

Christ is the answer only if He is made known as the answer. This knowledge is communicated by the Holy Spirit through human instrumentality. The communication must be by the Spirit. "The letter killeth, but the spirit giveth life."

A true theocentric view, therefore, not only recognizes God as Creator and Father but Jesus Christ as God's unique Son and our Lord and Savior. It likewise recognizes the Holy Spirit as God present and powerful. It is the Spirit who enables us to repent and to believe in Christ. It is the Spirit who enables us to grow in grace as believers. Effective service by Christians and effective unity between Christians are two of the Spirit's many gifts. Man's greatest need is to have his life centered on the eternal and Triune God.

As men are called to see the true centrality of God in all of life, there is new hope for planet earth.

Act on Your Hope

1. Consider what you now are doing to meet human needs—not only in your own community but around the world. Look at possible channels that are open to you. Decide whether or not you need to add to your present activities. Carry out your decision through prayer support, financial support, direct personal activities in which you can engage. These can include service to those in need where you are and also helping others to recognize and act on need.

2. Consider the extent to which you put Christ at the center of your life. Remember that Christian living is not simply a matter of having become a Christian at some time in the past. Day-by-day decisions should be made in light of Christ's will. Seek the leadership of the Holy Spirit; seek His power to act under His leadership.

8

Diligently Guard Unity

The Holy Spirit came to earth to carry on the work that Christ began—"to seek and to save that which was lost." The Spirit came to perpetuate what Christ came to initiate. Jesus spoke of this in John 16:7–11, pointing out that the Spirit should come following His ascension in order to "reprove the world of sin, and of righteousness, and of judgment."

As John Calvin truly emphasized, it is the Holy Spirit who calls men to repentance and faith, and it is only by the Spirit's calling that true repentance and faith are possible.

Yet there is a crucial truth that we must remember. The Spirit has made Himself dependent on human instrumentality. He has no body and has made Himself dependent on our bodies.

The Requirement of Unity

The Spirit depends on us. Christ entrusted the proclamation of His gospel to His church. This is why unity is required among Christians. How sorely is Christ being wounded in the house of His friends. How dreadfully is the lost world being left to its own fate. It is only as believers permit the Holy Spirit to minister through them that the work that Jesus came to initiate shall be effectively carried on by the Spirit.

For this work, unity is an unqualified requirement. No wonder Paul said that we are to give diligence to maintain the unity of the Spirit in the bond of peace. The Spirit calls all of us who are committed to Christ into unity of mind and purpose.

On several occasions Paul referred to the composition and function of the members of the natural body as illustrating the spiritual body of believers. Isn't the unity of the human body remarkable? We take God's miracles for granted. What a miracle that when a man puts his fork into his meat, it goes to his mouth instead of to his ear. I can hear someone say, "But I know a guy whose fork, when he eats, goes straight to his ear." I think I know the same fellow. But, he is in love! Usually the unity of the human body is miraculously smooth and effective.

A man touches his finger to a hot piece of metal. Instantly the finger sends a message to the brain: "It's hot down here!" The brain fires a message back: "Move it!" Like lightening, the finger is moved. What unity!

The work of Christ cannot be perpetuated except through the ministry of the Spirit of God. The Spirit of God cannot function except through committed believers.

The Spirit of God has baptized us as believers into a body whose Head is Christ. The unity of the Spirit is that glorious unity of all believers as various members of this spiritual body. Only believers can keep the unity of the Spirit, since only believers are members of this body of which Christ is the Head.

Paul says that we are to keep this unity of the Spirit "in the bond of peace." The bond of peace is Christ. "He is our peace." Therefore, the unity of the Spirit is possible only in Christ. Without Christ as Head, the church is dead. Years ago, Dr. Harold John Ockenga told me a startling fact about one of America's larger denominations. He said that this group had closed the doors of one of its churches on the average of every four days for the preceding twenty-five years. That is more than two thousand churches—as many as some smaller denominations claim. What's the matter? Christ was dethroned as Head.

The true unity produced by the Spirit is a similarity of nature in all believers who surrender to His control.

Now there can be unity that the Spirit of God does not own. Suppose that a church should vote unanimously to discontinue all gifts for outreach—missions and evangelism. Suppose that someone would then say, "Oh, what unity!" Yes, that is a form of unity, but it would not be the unity of the Spirit. The Holy Spirit would not act in this way. This would be a unity of freezing rather than of fusing. Objects stick together in subzero weather.

The work of the Spirit is different. First, He separates things are are not alike in nature, and then He unites those that are alike. Thus the fires of evangelism separate the true believers from the empty talkers. The believers are then united in the work of God.

The unity of the Spirit is promoted when the body of believers is led by the Spirit. Remember that the Holy Spirit came to perpetuate the work that Jesus came to initiate. And you can put it down as axiomatic that when there is no effort to bring men to faith in Jesus Christ, something is radically deficient in a group of people calling themselves Christians. The unity produced by the Spirit is active unity—a functional unity. It doesn't stem from human coercion but from the drawing power of the

Spirit. As men are drawn towards the Spirit, they are drawn towards each other. The unity of the Spirit is expressed as believers become instruments of the Holy Spirit in glorifying God through evangelism and edification.

Unity in Diversity

The unity of the Spirit is real in spite of trivial differences. It is a unity in diversity. The waves differ from each other, but the ocean is one. The branches differ, but the tree is one. The planets differ, but the solar system is one. The members differ, but the body is one.

My wife and I are contemplating no divorce. Though married for more than twenty-five years, I love her more today than ever before. The reason for this, however, is not uniformity of thought. We disagree on many things. It hurts me that she is so often wrong! When we have a disagreement, we sit down and discuss the problem. She tells me what she thinks. I tell her what I think. We compromise. We do what she thinks!

In a sermon several years ago, I said in substance, "I doubt that there has ever been a married couple with all their faculties who have lived together for a period of six months or more without a disagreement—expressed or unexpressed. It may be something that the one disagreeing has never revealed. It may be such a trivial thing as which one is the better driver. It may be disagreement over the proper room temperature. The husband may think that the room temperature ought to be 68 degrees Fahrenheit. The wife thinks it ought to be 140."

After the service, a tall, well-upholstered woman strode down the aisle towards me. She was holding the hand of a little, dried-up, "Mr. Casper Q. Milquetoast" sort of a husband, who meekly followed in her train. She rebuked me with gusto, saying, "Henry here and I have been married for 32 years, and we've never had a disagreement." I gulped and thought to myself, "I don't blame him! Self-preservation is a primal law of life!"

There are unmistakble manifestations of the unity of the Spirit.

There is the manifestation of lowliness. This is one of the characteristics of the normally functioning spiritual body. The word "lowliness" could be translated "modesty," that is, an utter lack of self-assertiveness. Self-assertiveness is the hallmark of immaturity. From childhood we begin to boast of our attainments and abilities. One of the first duties of a parent is to curb this tendency. As mature Christians, we need to be delivered from this self-assertiveness. We have nothing that we have not received. With what modesty we should behave! Nothing will puncture the balloon of spiritual egotism quite as quickly as the pin of crisis—overwhelming crisis for which human resources are not adequate.

I could not help but notice during the years of a high-flying economy how often men would subtly but unmistakably hint that their great business acumen had paid off in handsome profits. Many of those same men were a shambles after the economic setbacks of '69 and '70 had done their worst.

Those who are dominated by the Spirit of God don't get unduly elated when things go well nor unduly dejected when things go badly. Their joy is in the Lord and in the fact that their names are written down in the Lamb's Book of Life.

Meekness, Forbearing

Another manifestation of the normally functioning

spiritual body is meekness. The root of the original word used in Ephesians 4:2 means humility—a spirit that never takes offense.

Someone reviles us. We flare up. Why? Because we are not clad in the comely robe of meekness. They said of Jesus, "He has a devil." He endured it for "when he was reviled, reviled not again; when he suffered, he threatened not" (1 Pet. 2:23).

When a member of the spiritual body is functioning normally under the leadership of the Holy Spirit, praise and blame affect him the same. He is rightly related to a fellowman because he is rightly related to God. He stands in awe of no man, and he stands in condemnation of no man.

Another manifestation of the normally functioning spiritual body is long-suffering. This means "to endure with unruffled temper." "For what glory is it, if, when ye be buffeted for your faults, ye shall take it patiently? But if, when ye do well, and suffer for it, ye take it patiently, this is acceptable with God" (I Pet. 2:20).

Do you know much about long-suffering? You say, "Well, if what he said about me were true, I wouldn't mind; but I can't stand it when I know it is a miserable falsehood." The flesh talks like that. That doesn't come from the new nature—the Spirit nature—but from the old nature—the natural man.

Forbearing one another in love is another characteristic of the normally funcionting spiritual body.

Believers are not to resent injuries or retaliate for wrong done to them. Rather they are to bear with each other's infirmities and weaknesses.

This forbearing is not done from the motive of mere worldly courtesy or condescension or smug complacency or contemptuous indifference but from the love which "suffereth long and is kind." If the body is to function properly, there must a unity among its members. It must be a dynamic unity of which the Holy Spirit is the author. It must produce a harmony among believers. There is a harmony in the graveyard; everyone is dead. There is a harmony in a hospital; all the patients are sick. The harmony of the Spirit is the opposite of these.

In every other realm there must be competition—merchants for trade, lawyers for clients, doctors for patients, athletes for medals, scholars for awards. But there is no room for competition in God's work. The church's business is not to get but to give.

"Forbearing one another in love." What do you do when your thumb gets hurt? Do you strike it? Do the other members of the body "pile it on"? No! The whole body comes to the rescue. The hands feed the mouth. The feet carry the body. The eyes and the ears have their respective responsibilities. Which part of your body would you want to do without?

Family unity does not necessarily result from persons having the same name and living under the same roof. If their names are the same and yet their purposes adverse, if their characters are alien and their affections unlike, the very closeness of their activities will only increase their sense of disunion. A true family is one in purpose and feeling. Seas may separate them, the old home may be broken up, yet they will be one. Likewise all are one who worship God the Father revealed in His Son Jesus Christ and who draw their impulse and their aspirations from the one Spirit of holiness and love.

Said Chrysostom, the golden-mouthed, "Bind not the hands, but bind the heart and mind. Bind thyself to thy brother. They bear all things lightly who are bound together by love. Bind thyself to Him and Him to thee. For to this end was the Spirit given that He might unite those who are separated by station and diversity of habits: old and young, rich and poor, child, youth, and man, male, female and every soul become in a manner one, and more entirely so than if they were one body." There is power in unity. There is strength in concentration and harmony. The scriptures are not silent on this point.

Power for Good

At Babel God found that "the people are one." He said, "Now nothing will be restrained from them which they undertake to do." There is power in unity for evil. There is likewise power in unity for good.

Joshua had the people come together. He had them march together, blow the trumpets together, shout together. The walls of Jericho tumbled down.

Gideon had to thin the ranks down until he got a crowd that would work together. He said, "At the signal, everybody blow your bugles together and break your pitchers at once. Then all in one accord with one voice shout, 'The sword of the Lord and of Gideon.' "

The design and blueprint for all spiritually effective work is found in Acts 2:1, "When the day of Pentecost was fully come, they were all with one accord in one place." Fences and walls and ditches and gullies had not yet been improvised to scatter God's forces. But 120 in that upper room had heard Christ's prayer. They had heard Him say, just before He went to Gethsemane, "Father, make them one." Union among such people is understandable, but union among those of contrary philosophy is unthinkable. "Can two walk together except they be agreed?"

There is great power in this unity of the Spirit.

Centuries ago there was a small band of 300 in a cavalry unit of the Theban army. They proved a great terror to any enemy that they were called on to fight. They were companions who had bound themselves together by a vow of perpetual friendship. It was their purpose to stand together until the last drop of their blood was spilled upon the ground. Because of their unity, they were called a "sacred battalion." Affection for the state as well as fidelity for each other bound them together. They achieved marvels. Some of their accomplishments were fabulous.

What a name for the militant church—"The Sacred Battalion." It is when the church is thus animated by unity in the Spirit that she is victorious. Don't ever discount the reality of spiritual mathematics. One shall chase a thousand. Two shall put ten thousand to flight. What an incredible ratio. Think, then, how the work of God leaps forward when hundreds of believers, motivated by the Spirit of God, maintain that unity that results in the execution of His will.

Maintaining this unity is not optional. It's mandatory. The word "endeavoring" should be translated "give diligence." The word "keep" means to keep by guarding. How then may we give diligence to keep the unity of the Spirit?

We keep the unity of the Spirit only as we cooperate in attitude and action with His purpose. Once again, let us remember that the Spirit is here to perpetuate the work that Jesus came to initiate. There can be no maintenance of the unity of the Spirit that disregards winning the lost to Christ and building up Christians in the faith.

Paul wrote, "I beseech you therefore, brethren, by the mercies of God, that ye present your bodies a living sacrifice, holy, acceptable unto God" (Rom. 12:1).

We are to present our bodies a living sacrifice unto God. To whom are we to yield these bodies? Not to God the Father. He has no need of a body. Not to Christ the Son. He has His own glorious body. We are to yield our bodies to the Holy Spirit, who is the member of the Godhead at work in this world. He has come to the earth without a body. His only way of carrying on His work is through the dedicated bodies of believers. He uses a man like Peter to speak to a Cornelius. He uses a Philip to speak to an Ethiopian eunuch. He uses a fifteen-year-old girl to speak to Dr. John Sung.

Fracturing Unity

We maintain the unity of the Spirit only when we are completely yielded to the Lord. The man who refuses to be faithful in the stewardship of his money fractures the unity of the Spirit. His attitude and actions are incompatible with the expressed will of the Holy Spirit. The man who fails to witness fractures the unity of the Spirit. His attitude and actions are incompatible with the will of the Spirit. That young man whom God has selected for specialized Christian service but who has rejected in deference to status and shekels fractures the unity of the Spirit. Obviously, his attitude and actions are incompatible with the will of the Spirit.

Several years ago my family accompanied me on a trip by car to a citywide crusade I was to conduct in Mobile, Alabama. It was July 4. We were driving through Tennessee and stopped to eat lunch in a hotel dining room in Clarksville. My son, then only seven years old, was in braces. He is a cerebral palsy victim, and he has difficulty in swallowing. Consequently, Christine, my wife, has to feed him. He was seated on her lap in his braces, and we were eating quietly. Of course, the very condition of my son occasioned a great deal of attention.

Soon I was aware of a young army captain walking up to the table. He looked at Johnny and then he looked at me. Tears welled in his eyes and spilled out on flushed cheeks. With trembling lips and a tremulous voice he said, "Mister, if you don't mind, I should like to give this to your little boy. I've had it for a long time, and it's protected my life many times in battle." Undoing his collar button and loosening his tie, he reached to a chain around his neck on which was a little insignia.

I said to him, "Son, our hope is in the Lord."

He countered, "If you don't mind, Sir, I should like to do this." Wise or unwise, I made no further efforts to dissuade him but rather let him follow the dictates of his heart. I shall never forget with what tenderness he placed the little chain around Johnny's neck. It was the captain's most precious possession.

I asked the paratrooper his name, but he was off instantly, obviously choked with emotion. Our appetites fled. We brought the meal to a premature conclusion, went out to the car, packed up Johnny's wheelchair, and drove down the highway. We had driven 200 hundred miles, and not a word had been said. That's a little unusual in our family. We were all "full," and then my wife broke the brittle air with a statement something like this, "What a rebuke that young officer administers to our apathy."

I asked her what she meant.

She said, "Here was a young officer who came to enjoy a holiday dinner with two of his buddies. He looked across the span of that hotel dining room and saw a little boy he had never seen before. The boy's need elicited his highest compassion. Unashamed of his tears and what his companions might say, he got up from his table, came over to the little stranger, and gave what he honestly believed was his most priceless possession—a possession he was convinced would definitely help the little boy."

She continued, "We say we love the Lord and that we maintain the unity of the Spirit. We say the Holy Spirit can work only through us in the winning of the lost to Christ. Yet there are people all about us on the block where we live, people who suffer not from physical but from spiritual cerebral palsy. We know we have the answer, yet we have been negligent in praying for them. Some of them we have never witnessed to."

The point was well-taken, and I have never forgotten it. There are multitudes of people in nations all around the world whom we have never seen but whom we ought to love if we are really motivated by the Holy Spirit of God. The answer for this poor world, sick with sin and paralyzed by fear, is the unity of the Spirit. Believers walking under the leadership of the Holy Spirit, carrying out His purpose in glorifying God, will witness the salvation of the lost and the building up of the saints.

Union per se is not the answer. Unity is—the unity of the Spirit—the unity of those who see God at the center of His world, Christ as Lord and Savior, and the Holy Spirit as the presence and power of God for salvation and effective service.

Unity of the Spirit, observed by believers, guarantees new hope for planet earth.

Act on Your Hope

1. Evaluate your attitude towards other Christians. Do you see mainly their strengths or their weaknesses, their virtues or their failings? Do you thank God for all of those

Dr. Haggai and Dr. E. H. Watson, Dean of Haggai Institute, Singapore

who truly love Jesus Christ as their Lord and Savior? Do you have a sense of unity with all believers? If not, ask yourself why. Consider how you may need to change your viewpoint.

2. Evaluate the attitude of your church towards other Christian bodies. Does it see itself as part of the total body of Christ, made up of all who have committed themselves to Him? Does it see that both the poor and the rich can belong to Christ's body, both the ignorant and the educated? Does it see that Christ has His people in all of the Christian denominational groups—Catholic, Protestant, Orthodox, and Pentecostal? Does it recognize the truth of Revelation 7:9, "I beheld, and, lo, a great multitude, which no man could number, of all nations, and kindreds, and people, and tongues, stood before the throne, and before the Lamb, clothed with white robes." Consider how you might help your church expand its vision of Christ's true body.

9

Is God a National God?

There is a grave temptation for Americans to identify God's priorities with America's national interests. This fact leaks out in the subtleties of conversation—in patronizing remarks about non-Western peoples, in belittling the need for Christian work overseas, in the superior air regarding our alleged surpassing methodology.

I have more reason to thank God for America than most who read this book. This glorious country provided a haven for my father when he fled from the oppression of the Turks in 1912. I don't take kindly to people who accuse me of being a wild-eyed, right-wing extremist simply because I love the flag and believe in the American Constitution. However, it is a sin against God, an assault upon the intelligence, and a betrayal of America's best interests to imply that God is a national God.

It is true there seems to have been a special relationship that God assumed toward America during the young life of this republic. There is no nation in history that's been lavished with such blessings as America has enjoyed. This makes America all the more culpable. "It shall be more tolerable for the land of Sodom in the day of judgment, than for thee" (Matt. 11:24). But because that is true—

since Capernaum has enjoyed so much more "light" than Sodom—how much more true it must be of America's "no excuse" position.

Christians East and West

The percentage of professing Christians in America is doubtlessly higher than in most areas of the world. To say that America is more Christian strains the point. Take Korea for example. The church bells ring in Taegu and Pusan and Seoul and other cities, large and small, early each morning. They ring at four o'clock and then again at four-thirty to remind the people of the five o'clock dawn prayer meetings in the churches. Six thousand churches in the Republic of Korea observe these early morning prayer meetings. I have seen as many as a thousand people on their knees for an hour in the predawn morning.

When a man is called a Christian in the United States, little is implied about his commitments. Is he a person who has yielded his life totally to Jesus Christ? Is he a liberal who scoffs at the efficacy of Christ's shed blood, views the Bible as no more inspired than Socrates' philosophy, and ridicules the bodily resurrection of Jesus from the grave? Or is he one who would profess Christian truths but shows by his life a total indifference to their demands?

Such ambiguity is not known in Korea. Ten percent of the population of the Republic of Korea is Christian. And, when I say Christian, I'm referring to committed believers in the person of Jesus Christ. Thirty percent of the military is reputedly Christian, as is forty-five percent of the Air Force.

It has been interesting to note that Korean soldiers serving in Vietnam have not become hooked on drugs as have so many of our boys. I can only conclude that the reason is a commitment to Jesus Christ. Korean Christians discipline themselves to reject anything that they recognize as potentially harmful to the body, the temple of the Holy Spirit.

There are many other nations in whose corporate life God is working in a remarkable way. I only use Korea as an example. Throughout history, God has assumed a special relationship to specific nations, usually on the basis of the relationship of those who name His name to Himself.

God and the Nations

There is value in tracing the working of God through the lives of various nations.

The center of Christian enterprise and outreach for the first fifty years after Christ's ascension was Jerusalem. Antioch in Syria was the center during the next fifty years. During the second and third centuries the nerve centers of Christian activity and outreach were Alexandria and Ephesus. From 330 until 600 the emphasis was in Constantinople. Then from 600 to 1050 the heart of Christian activity was in Rome. There was another move during the twelfth, thirteenth, and fourteenth centuries to other parts of Europe, such as France—especially when the papacy was located in Avignon.

The center of Christian activity and outreach during the sixteenth century was in Germany and Switzerland. During the seventeenth and eighteenth centuries Spain and Portugal sent out missionaries across the world. Great Britain was the birthplace of the modern missions movement late in the eighteenth century, and any thinking person will recognize the United States as the base for more Christian activity during the first half of the twentieth century than any other place.

History makes clear that God forsakes a nation when the nation forsakes God. He does not want it this way, but He will not burglarize human wills nor automate man's obedience and loyalty. He leaves when asked to leave.

Another observation is the fact that it was those claiming to be His children who thrust Him out from their respective areas. This has been done in many different ways. The legalism of the Old Testament has been grafted onto the revelation of grace personified in Jesus Christ. Sordid sensuality and worldliness have arisen. The essential nature of Christ has been denied, as in the case of the Gnostics at an early date and of the Unitarians in recent centuries. Unholy weldock has united the church and the state. Christ's command regarding world evangelization has been ignored. There have been divisive debates on interpreting the Bible and a decay in biblical theology. In short, loyalty to Christ as Lord has diminished, and human ego has mounted the throne. This ego demonstrates itself in humanism, universalism, liberalism, and syncretism. The human will is imposed upon the will of God.

Another interesting observation is that the general direction of this movement over the last two millennia has been from east to west. Many believe that Asia and the South Pacific will be the great centers of Christian activity and outreach during the coming decades. Surely there is great evidence for such an assumption. Louis Cassels of United Press International wrote that in one two-year period, two and a half million people turned to Christianity in the country of Indonesia alone. This is unprecedented in any nation during any two-year period in the history of Christianity.

Of course, there also are great revivals taking place in South Korea.

A Call for Stewardship

For the Asian nations to measure up to their opportunities in Christ, a new and biblically-based habit of financial stewardship will be required. There are some areas where the Christians understand this. However, many sincere believers in that part of the world—poverty-stricken to be sure—still look to the West for their financial requirements. Some of this is doubtlessly due to the paternalism of Western missions and the failure of Western Christians to teach what the Bible has to say about stewardship. The Lord's provisions have never been dependent upon a nation's gross national product or an individual's personal worth. Christ said, "Give, and it shall be given unto you; good measure, pressed down, and shaken together, and running over, shall men give into your bosom. For with the same measure that ye mete withal it shall be measured to you again" (Luke 6:38).

This is true in every area among every people. It is true as stated and is not to be spiritualized so as to rob it of the monetary and temporal application.

The Malaysia Evangelistic Fellowship, headed by Dr. G. D. James of Singapore, maintains an effective ministry across the world with virtually no Western financial help. The Presbyterians of Korea have built some of the most impressive churches and Christian institutions in the world, and they have done it without significant Western help. The current budget of the Young Nak Presbyterian Church in Seoul is the equivalent of a million American dollars. Compare the average per family income of Seoul with the average of my home city of Atlanta. A budget of more than fifteen million dollars would be required there for equal stewardship commitment.

Sadly, in days gone by, capable Asian leaders have subordinated their superior gifts and ministries in order not to offend the Westerners. Let it be said that the Westerners have ministered out of hearts of love. But, as we shall see in a later chapter, they fail to comprehend the Eastern mentality. Consequently, what was really an expression of love and concern and outgoingness appeared to the Easterners as arrogance and effrontery.

Evangelism International, the organization with which I work, is committed to the policy of "geographical integrity." Geographical integrity simply means that Christians of each area support with personnel, material, and finances the projects in their area. Korea has held major crusades in which I have been honored to be the evangelist. Korean Christians covered all their expenses. At our early Total Evangelism—Plus Project in Indonesia, the Indonesians—who were coming out of great poverty at the time —covered a great percentage of the total cost. They provided hundreds of people for the various leadership positions. This has continued to be true of our subsequent crusades there.

The Indonesian crusades have demonstrated great spiritual maturity and evangelistic passion. The first was the first time in the history of that country that the Presbyterians and the Pentecostals (along with other Christians) cooperated in one great united effort. As a result, glorious friendships were born and new understandings were created.

Not With Observation

Jesus said, "The kingdom of God cometh not with observation." This has been true historically. The great movements of God have had small and unobserved beginnings. They have grown up like the mustard seed, without observation. On the other hand, loud and grand beginnings, summoning as with the sound of a trumpet the whole world to behold what a mighty birth is at hand or what a glorious thing it is when born, have almost surely come to nothing.

With the advent of stereophonic sound, hoopla techniques, and Madison Avenue image-building capabilities, it has become possible to simulate the results of Pentecost. Unfortunately, there are those who erroneously assume that the Holy Spirit—the cause of Pentecost—has therefore been present. Perhaps this is one of the explanations for the moral dualism we see in the West. On the one hand, we have more gospel broadcasts, more high-priced telecasts, more Christian publications, more evangelical schools and institutions than ever before. Yet there is not one American city of size that does not have certain areas where a person walks at night in jeopardy of his life.

We have become so celebrity conscious in the West that we have made the programs of Christian outreach dependent too often on the appearance of some celebrated personage. This is fine if the person has had a real experience of grace. Where such experience is absent, it is a disgrace to the Lord and a weakening factor in the impact of God's message. How unthinkable it would have been for John the Baptist to have insisted that Herod introduce him before he ministered. How unthinkable that Paul the Apostle would have insisted that Nero give him the key to the city and "say a good word" before he ministered in Rome!

It is still true that, "The foolishness of God is wiser than men; and the weakness of God is stronger than men. For ye see your calling, brethren, how that not many wise men after the flesh, not many mighty, not many noble, are called: But . . . God hath chosen the weak things of the world to confound the things which are mighty; and base things of the world, and things which are dispised, hath God chosen, yea, and things which are not, to bring to nought things that are: That no flesh should glory in his presence. But of him are ye in Christ Jesus, who of God is made unto us wisdom, and righteousness, and sanctification, and redemption: That, according as it is written, He that glorieth, let him glory in the Lord" (I Cor. 1:25–31) .

There is something refreshing among Christians of the Third World. These believers do not seem to have the mania for identifying the work of the Lord with that which is accepted and popular among those in the power structure. They do not require approval by those who constitute some particular "in" crowd. Christian work in the Orient so often must be understood in terms of people like John Sung in Southeast Asia and Sadhu Sunder Singh in India. These are men whose greatness lay not in the eyes of men but of perceptive Christians.

Indonesia has been the site of the greatest revival in the history of Christianity. This revival cannot be traced to any single individual or to any single group. Revival has continued now for nineteen years. It is a movement of the Spirit of God. It has been like the wind—heard but not seen. You can't tell "whence it cometh or whither it goeth."

Over thirty years ago more than 5,000 evangelistic teams were formed by John Sung. Each team was composed of three men. These men literally blanketed the area then known as the Dutch East Indies. Whoever heard of them? Who are they? Where were they from? What was their background? "It is the glory of God to conceal the matter."

Two thousand years ago how little did imperial Rome, enthroned in her golden palaces, amusing herself in her bloody amphitheaters, dream that she nourished within her bosom a mightier than herself? Hidden from her sight was a weakness which would be stronger than all her strength. It was a foolishness which would be wiser than all her wisdom, a patience which would weary all her cruelty, a love which would vanquish all her hate. I note in those areas where multitudes are turning to Christ an absence of concern for credit or desire for prominence. There is a refreshing no-return motivation to make Christ known. We must ever thank God for all of the technological advance and use these gifts to serve His purposes. The danger to be avoided is in seeking to make technology and methodology supreme, leaving vital godliness to be secondary.

To quote the great Bible scholar Meyer, "The kingdom of God cometh not with vulgar and physical visibility." It cometh not with pomp and fanfare.

I see one frightening trend. With the glamorization and secularization of Christian outreach, there is a rise in antinomianism. This is the assumption that Christians are above the moral law. By contrast, Christians of the third world—the Orient, Mideast, and Africa—take a much more serious look at the Ten Commandments. While they are not legalists, they recognize that grace did not abrogate the law. Rather, it fulfilled the law. The rising antinomianism in some Christian circles of America and Europe is shocking. Antinomianism says that since you are saved by grace, you can live any way that you want. There are no restrictions; all is fine. There is a breakdown in observance of the Lord's Day, a relaxed standard regarding divorce and adultery, a de-emphasis on the importance of home relationships, and a non-biblical embrace of deception.

Misnomer of the Century

People of the non-West nations are not rejecting Jesus Christ so much as they are rejecting Westernization. Unfortunately, they have been led to believe that Christianity is a Western religion. Westerners, of course, have given Christianity prominence. They also have tended to press Western customs and habit patterns on converts that have nothing to do with Christianity.

For example, a hundred years ago a missionary went to a certain area of the South Pacific. The natives were practically nude. The missionary taught that if a woman was committed to Christ, she would wear her dress as high as her neck and as low as her feet. Today, people representing the same mission come to that area in miniskirts and hot pants. As the nationals dispose of the old dress, they tend to dispose of the "Christianity" that it supposedly typified. As unfortunate as this is, it is a glaring illustration of affixing to the gospel cultural trappings that the Bible does not endorse.

Here is another example. In 1935 the Baptist World Alliance met in Berlin, Germany. Baptist women from the Southern states felt no inconsistency at all in using cosmetics. They saw no violation of their Christian witness. When they arrived in Berlin, some of the German women were greatly exercised over the "make-up" worn by the Americans. They questioned their spirituality. At the same time, the German women saw no inconsistency in drinking beer and wine, which was unthinkable to the Southern women. Here were two western nations with diverse customs. The German women were committed Christians, as were the women from the American South. Each ran the risk of erroneous conclusions based on outward symbols rather than on the unseen commitment of the heart.

I always enjoy reminding my Asian friends that Christ was an Asian. He was born in Asia. His mother was an Asian. He lived, ministered, suffered, died, and was buried in Asia. It was in Asia that He rose from the grave and ascended back to heaven. It will be to Asia that he will come again!

One of the reasons people overseas consider Christianity a Western religion is because Christians from the West have rejected native music, art forms, and literature. They have forced the gospel of Christ into a Western mold, a Western style. When they came to Asia, they translated English and German hymns, paying practically no attention to the power of indigenous music. They required the new Christians to praise God in Christ through translated hymns rather than seeking to develop words and music suited to the existing cultures. The pictures used in illustrating gospel stories were of Westerners! (How often even today we see Jesus represented with blue eyes and blond hair—a true Germanic type!)

As I have said before, I am the second generation product of Western missions. I thank God for them. But how often missionaries have failed to see the implications of their approaches.

There is a rising tide of nationalism in third-world nations. Well there should be. I have grave questions about a man, under ordinary circumstances, who does not place his country above all other countries in his estimation and love. I can understand the Irishman who was asked, "What is your nationality?"

"I'm an Irishman."

"What would you be if you were not an Irishman?"

"I'd be ashamed of myself!"

In less than a century, a great percentage of the people of Korea have turned to Christ. No other non-Western nation equals it in that regard. Part of the reason must inevitably be attributed to the fact that Presbyterians in Korea understood the importance of decolonizing and de-Westernizing the gospel. This goes back to early leaders, including Dr. Sam Moffett, two of whose sons still work there. Under the influence of missionary statesman John Nevius from China, the leaders in Korea recognized that Paul the Apostle did not export from Jerusalem to Europe organizational formats, social structures, or leadership personnel.

The Presbyterian church in Korea is truly a Korean church—Korean leadership, Korean organization, Korean structures, and Korean funding. In that small nation the Presbyterians alone have won to faith in Christ more than 1,300,000 people since 1886. There are other marvelous victories for Christ there among peoples of other denominations, including Southern Baptists, the Assemblies of God, the Methodists, and many others. The Presbyterians, however, are the oldest and strongest of the Protestant bodies.

The Mar Thoma Church in India gives great signs of strength and future growth. According to tradition, it was founded by the Apostle Thomas in A.D. 52. This is another group that has retained its own national characteristics and culture in the execution of its worship and in the outreach of its witness.

Antoine Deeb is a Syrian whose ministry across the Mideast nations is uniques and without peer. A young man near thirty, he has been gifted by God with outstanding singing and speaking ability. One of the great personal thrills of my life is to hear this man sing the gospel in his native Arabic to indigenous Syrian tunes. He can sing Western songs, and sing them well. He would be a smash in any church across the United States or Canada. In dealing with the Asians, however, he employs Asian customs and cultural patterns. It's no wonder that God is so singularly using this dedicated young man—the George Whitefield of the Arab world.

God is concerned with nations, but nations also need to be concerned with God. No nation can have a monopoly on God, but God will bless any nation whose people seek and honor His will as revealed by Christ and declared through the Holy Spirit. Is God still the God of America? He is willing, but are we? In no case, however, is He exclusively the God of the West. When all believers—East and West—see this, there is new hope for planet earth.

Act on Your Hope

1. Pray for a revival of Christian commitment in America. Remember that America has no monopoly on Christ or His blessings, that fullest blessing depends on repentance and commitment.

2. Pray that American Christians may regain a wide vision of the stewardship to the gospel—that those who know the truth are obligated to share it. Recognize that America today is in deep spiritual need, that many professing Christians exhibit no sense of the urgency of the gospel.

10

Rejoice in Encouraging Indicators

It appears that the great powers are on a collision course in the Mideast. World inflation threatens the future security of the world's people. Pollution and the population explosion spell imminent doom. Yet there are some greatly encouraging indicators.

A short while ago, the Rev. David Wilkerson attended a service I was conducting in Covina, California. When I recognized him in the congregation, I asked him to come to the platform to speak to the people for a few minutes. When he did, he made the prediction that we possibly could be on the threshold of the greatest spiritual revival in American history. He asserted his conviction that it would begin among the young people. I find myself in agreement with him.

Not too many years ago one could not speak of Jesus Christ on most college campuses and get a hearing. Today the name itself—the name Jesus—occasions instant interest.

Two Crusades in Portugal

In Portugal God is doing a great work, and multitudes

are turning to the Lord. It has been my privilege under God to lead two massive crusades there, first in 1970 and again in 1972. Here are some excerpts from a write-up in the *Methodist Recorder* of London regarding the 1970 crusade. The headline reads, "Full houses for Portugal crusade." The story says, "Three regular members of the congregation of the Mirante Methodist church, Oporto, Portugal, one a Portuguese, one a Swiss and one an Indonesian, (the wives of the two latter being, respectively, Italian and German!), were prime movers in a recent evangelistic campaign held in Oporto, promoted by the Christian Business Men's Association, which brought together nightly for more than a week over 1,000 in the cinema at Vila Nova de Gaia, the adjacent city to Oporto, just across the River Douro.

"Each night many had to be turned away, and on the last night, when a little latitude was given by the authorities, some hundreds stood round the walls. Almost a hundred years ago, a few yards away, James Cassells . . . was stoned for preaching the Gospel near to where he constructed, in 1868, what was the first Wesleyan Methodist chapel in Portugal!

"The visiting evangelist was Dr. John Haggai, of Evangelism International, of Atlanta, Georgia, USA, who presented a Bible-based evangelical message in a reasoned, attractive and practical manner which captured and held the interest and attention not only of the avowed Christians present, but of the undecided, the indifferent, the agnostic and even the atheist, who were there each night in no small numbers.

"Many people responded to the appeals for decision made each night, and are now in large numbers to be found in the churches which are caring for them. . . .

"There was, however, no proselytising in the preaching, only an objective statement of the Christian message; and never a negative emphasis, as might be testified by the fact that at the final meeting, when people were invited to raise their hands to indicate their desire for prayer to be made for them, one RC priest raised his hand in request.

"The campaign had the support of all the pastors of the various Evangelical denominations in the area, both in the preparatory period, when nightly meetings were held in local churches, at which the speakers were visiting business men from the USA, and on the platform at the campaign meetings. The choirs of the Mirante Methodist church and the Oporto Pentecostal church sang on alternate nights, coming together . . . for the final meeting."

This story ran April 9, 1970, along with a photograph showing Portuguese Methodist leader Albert Aspey and me.

The 1970 meetings we conducted in Portugal were the first public meetings ever permitted for non-Catholic evangelistic witness in public buildings of that great country. There were some interesting sidelights. Any public gathering in Portugal must provide a fifteen-minute interval at the end of one hour. Also, no one under twelve years of age is permitted to attend except on Saturday and Sunday. A further restriction was that only those with tickets stamped for the day and with the seat and aisle would be permitted entrance. By the end of the crusades in both Oporto and Lisbon (where crowds passed the 8,000 mark) the police and firemen themselves were so involved and interested that they permitted standees to come in after all the seats were taken. Roman Catholic priests attending the meetings wrote up the services, and the articles appeared in Portugal's leading papers.

Please Preach Longer

After I had preached in Lisbon three nights, the Committee asked to see me. They told me they were disappointed in only one matter, and I asked them what that was. They said, "The Lord has brought you a long way, and this is an unprecedented opportunity. You don't preach long enough." I was astounded. Nobody in America ever made that kind of accusation! The messages had been lasting about forty-five minutes. They requested that I plan no less than an hour and a half!

The first part of the service, after that, continued for about forty-five minutes. Then there was the recess called for by the Portuguese law. The people attending the services immediately ran out to get coffee or brandy. In exactly fifteen minutes they would be worshipfully silent in their seats to listen for the rest of the time.

The victories of that crusade rewarded the hearts of two non-Portuguese—a man from Holland and his wife, who had come from Switzerland. For fifteen years they had prayed and prepared for this effort. The largest cooperating group was Pentecostal.

Each of the firemen and the policemen designated by the government to supervise the services in Oporto bought new Bibles. They brought them to me to be autographed at the close of the last service. It was a moving experience to watch them carefully take off the newspaper wrappers which they used to protect their Bibles.

The maitre d' of the hotel where we stayed was converted. He had studied for the priesthood for four years but had not continued due to severe tragedies in his life. The glow on his face gave expression to the new joy in his heart. An army major came to the crusade in Oporto and was under great conviction. Because of complications involving his military record, he felt he could not profess faith in Christ. Without telling us, he moved to Lisbon in order to attend the very first service there. At the invitation he was the first to step forward and gave evidence of genuine conversion.

The owner of a textile factory in Coimbra brought a bus load at her own expense to Oporto. She explained that only non-Christians had been permitted to ride the chartered bus. Many of this group came to know the Lord.

The crusade of 1970 was followed by one in 1972 marked by even larger response. The total estimated attendance in 1970 was 53,000. In 1972 it was twenty-five percent larger. More than 2,000 people were brought to Christ in this second crusade, and conversions continued to be reported during the follow-up meetings that were held by local religious leaders. There were more than two hundred counselors to meet with the new converts following their public decisions. More than half of these had been converted themselves during the 1970 crusade.

The second crusade was marked by striking support from public officials. Some of the restrictive laws, such as those forbidding school children to attend a public meeting during the week and the requirement for the intermission after the first hour, were lifted by special permission.

My decision to accept the invitation to go to Portugal grew out of my desire to go where the need is greatest. Apparently, I was the only evangelist that was acceptable to all of the sponsoring groups. I also believe that my Syrian ancestry helped to open the door. The Portuguese people have Syrian blood. This seems to have been a factor in acceptance.

I was the first evangelical preacher ever to be granted an

audience by His Eminence, Dom Antonio Cardinal Ribeiro, Patriarch of Lisbon, the head of the nation's Catholic Church. He surprised me—and my host, Mr. M. Van den Heuvel—by indicating that he had attended the first crusade. Among other things, Cardinal Ribeiro said, "We, too, look for the return of our Lord and Savior, Jesus Christ."

I see evidence that God is doing a great work in Portugal. This lies not only in the response to the two crusades but from contacts with Catholic leaders. Many Portuguese Catholics have a consuming interest in Bible study, Christian growth, and evangelism. New recognition is being given to the laity. A distinction is being made between nominal mental asent to the truths of the Scripture and a vital personal relationship to Jesus Christ. It is inevitable that in the wake of this spiritual renewal there will come industrial progress and benefits to society. Historically, this has always been true.

In Kuwait some key leaders have come to know the Lord through the reading of the Bible and the witness of an outstanding Arab Christian leader whose name I withhold by request. To fully appreciate such events, it is necessary to remember the strong resistence to Christianity in Arab and other strongly Muslim areas. Community pressures against conversion have held back all but the most committed. God today, however, is winning fresh victories over such strong opposition.

Starting in 1970, many Christian leaders in Assam, a northeastern state of India, have been involved in a project they call Operation St. Paul. Three of Assam's Christian leaders were trained at Evangelism International's Haggai Institute. They returned to Assam and transferred their training to 193 other Christian leaders. These in turn have

Dr. Haggai preaching at Jakarta, Indonesia

all become involved in Operation St. Paul. What makes this so strategic is the fact that white "preaching" missionaries have been expelled from Asam. The last one, an Australian Baptist, was expelled in September, 1970.

In Australia, Baptists are increasing faster than the population of the country.

In Indonesia, as I have indicated, God is doing an unprececented work. Let me share with you the report made in *Eternity* magazine in January, 1970. The writer is Mr. Paul Purukan, himself an Indonesian: "Four thousand men and women made decisions for Christ, and 5,000 others enrolled to the Good News Bible course. More than 100 thousand people heard the gospel and 600 thousand received portions of the Scriptures and tracts.

" 'The crusade story is much too important to be overlooked,' a newspaper editor commented. 'Something phenomenal is happening, affecting the spiritual life of thousands of people.' Such was the impact of the three-week Java crusade which began in the nation's capital October 3.

"Jakarta, with four and a half million inhabitants, is in many ways an incredible city. Newly-built skyscrapers decorate Jalan Thamrin and many other highways. The boulevards are jammed with Mercedes and Impalas, driven by American, German, Japanese and other foreign businessmen. The city is becoming a thriving commercial center in Southeast Asia.

"And yet, for all these superlative qualities, the city still has its old problems.

"Thousands of struggling, helpless victims of poverty sleep in streets, in parks, even in Monas square in front of the presidential palace. Ironically, there are thriving sections like Menteng and Kebayoran, but in many places there are slums with people living in extreme poverty, even in the heart of the city."

Purukan goes on to tell of the material and of the spiritual need in his nation, which, with a population of 125 million, is the fifth most populous one in the world. Indonesia has 110 million Muslims, making it the world's largest Muslim nation. Yet the religious life of the people is more traditional and cultural than vital. In spite of centuries of Dutch colonial influence, Christianity has offered very little witness in the past. The article goes on: "To offset this failure, concerned church leaders held a seminar on evangelism in Tretes, East Java, in March 1969. The 183 Indonesian ministers and evangelists attending the seminar unanimously resolved to launch a massive soul-winning crusade. An interdenominational committee was set up to make the necessary preparations. Dr. John Haggai of Atlanta, Georgia, who organized the seminar, was asked to lead the crusade to be conducted in Java first.

"A frequent visitor to Indonesia, this was Dr. Haggai's third major evangelistic undertaking in this country. In May last year, he led a group of 57 American ministers and evangelists conducting simultaneous meetings in 50

Protestant churches in Jakarta. Among the group were Merv Rosell, Earnest Watson, Hubert Mitchell and Jerry Beavan.

"The crusade brought together an estimated 1,000 Christians who volunteered to serve as Bible instructors, counselors, ushers and choir members. Laymen were united as never before in mustering their forces for the greatest evangelistic thrust ever held in this city. . . .

"On the first night 5,000 people turned out. The majority were Christians. Recalcitrant ministers, who the month before were unconvinced that the crusade would do any good, changed their minds and urged their people to go. On the second night the attendance increased to 6,500, and it held at that figure night after night. Up to the end of the ten-day campaign more than 65,000 people attended and just over 2,700 responded to the invitation. These included bank presidents, a movie actress, and even underworld hoods and prostitutes."

This campaign in Jakarta was followed by one in Surabaya, capital of East Java. Here attendance was more than 10,000 in each service, and 1,200 confessed faith in Christ. Purukan says, "Never before have so many Moselms been won to faith a Christ by a single soul-winning effort."

On Waikiki Beach thousands of people are introduced to Christ through the ministry of Bob Turnbull. It is a fresh, relevant, and updated approach that centers squarely in the person of Jesus Christ.

Christian groups in South India are deploying missionaries into areas of North India. Thirty-five percent of the people in the state of Kerala (in South India) are professing Christians, while not quite one percent of the people in the state of Punjab profess Christianity.

In Africa there is a great turning to God in many areas.

A Presbyterian church announces worship service attendance in excess of twenty thousand. What makes this so remarkable is that so many of the people have to walk for hours just to get there.

South of the border, in Central and South America, God is moving in a mighty way. One of His outstanding spokesmen is Luis Palau, whose ministry is reaching tens of thousands in the nations of this area.

I have mentioned Korea a number of times in this book, but I want to conclude this chapter by saying a word concerning the crusade there in which I participated in 1972. In three weeks, according to the sponsoring organization, more than 31,000 decisions for Christ were made. I have never seen such a great response to the gospel anywhere else in the world.

There is thus a rising tide of Christian evangelization around the world. In many places, the Holy Spirit is at work, empowering his people and convicting the lost. Christians of America should renew their commitment to Christ and pray for the outpouring of spiritual victories evident in so many other areas. This is a time for hope. It is a time for prayer. The great revival in Korea has been going on for more than 65 years. I cannot help but attribute it to the place of prayer in the lives of the Korean believers. Earlier, I mentioned the early morning prayer services that are held throughout the nation of South Korea. A significant portion of the regular church services is also devoted to prayer. At one particular church, between 2,000 and 3,000 people gather every Tuesday to pray from 10 o'clock until 4 o'clock the next morning. It's no wonder that God is blessing with tremendous victory and power. In the words of Dr. Donald McGavran, authority on world missions and church growth, "Great

President Soeharto of Indonesia greets Dr. Haggai during 1969 Crusade

expectations and great prayers are conducive to church growth."

Act on Your Hope

1. Pray for revival in the nations of the world. Pray for one specific nation as suggested in chapter 5, but add to this other nations in other parts of the world.

2. Pray for specific evangelistic efforts as you learn of them, such as the overseas crusades sponsored by Evangelism International.

11

Reject Cultural Colonialism

In Bombay one of India's leading citizens, holding a responsible position in the government, told me that a bill was then before Parliament which, if passed, would make it illegal for anybody in India to receive financial assistance from any Christian organization outside of India. So far as I know, this bill has not passed, but the reports are that it is not "dead." When you understand that a reputed ten percent of India's gross national product comes from overseas Christian organizations and remember India's great financial needs, you begin to see a striking picture. There is a keen resistance by many of India's people to Westernization. I am firmly convinced that the reaction is not to Jesus Christ but to Westernization.

Let me say parenthetically that India is to be commended for her sacrificial assistance to the refugees from Bangladesh. Events surrounding the birth of Bangladesh were highly tragic, and India responded in a humanitarian fashion.

To return to the point, peoples of the East are now feeling and expressing strong resentment towards the West. An Asian friend, a respected evangelical leader with an earned Th.D., has said to me, "To put it in American parlance, I must tell you that the American Christian organizations are 'bombing out' in Southeast Asia because they do not understand the Eastern mentality. Their motivation is God-glorifying, but their methods are deplorable."

Non-West nations have a totally different attitude toward the West than they demonstrated twenty years ago. This is understandable. They feel that America and the western European nations, while discarding political colonialism, are nevertheless fostering and sponsoring a business and cultural colonialism. They do not stand in awe of the Western nations as they once did. The three nations with the fastest rate of growth in gross national product today are all in Asia, not in the West.

A View from the East

Singapore is throbbing and growing at a dizzying pace. The growth rate according to its illustrious Prime Minister, Lee Kuan Yew, is more than nine percent a year. Thirty-three hotels with nearly 10,000 rooms have been opened recently. A new apartment is built every thirty-six minutes in urban renewal projects, and Singapore's harbor is soon to be the world's third largest. Ships from all six continents wait for space. The nation's oil refineries turn out 400,000 barrels a day.

No wonder Singapore can be choosy about encouraging people to locate there.

The streets are safer in Singapore than are those of any city of comparable size in America, and the city is one of the cleanest of its size in the world—perhaps the cleanest. Throwing a cigarette into a roadside drain can draw a penalty of up to $500 U.S. and an imprisonment of up to two months. A dirty car exhaust that contributes to pollution can get the car owner a 90-day holiday in jail. The fact that life insurance actuaries estimate the life span of Singaporeans as sixty-six years tells something about Singapore's success in eliminating disease and sponsoring cleanliness.

This city, which rejects films displaying bare bosoms and bald violence, takes a dim view of many of the movies coming out of western Europe and the United States. This city with its "Rugged Society" rejects as demoralizing and degenerative the permissiveness of the West. For example, excessively long hair on boys or men is not tolerated.

It ill behooves a Westerner to go to Singapore or similar centers of the East with the presumptuous step of a "know it all." Actually, many Singaporeans look upon the West as decadent. If the Westerner proposes peace through Christ, some Singaporeans are perplexed, even though their Eastern hospitality and graciousness keep them from saying so. They well know that the West is marked by disrespect for parents, the drug epidemic, the meteorically rising crime rate, galloping inflation, the growing pollution problem, and a fantastic divorce rate. Is it any wonder that Singaporeans question the right of a Westerner to lecture tham?

Easterners resent, and justifiably so, Westerners talking about providing training for national leadership—using Westerners to do the training, employing Western-producing materials (printed on Western presses), and using the Western "cookbook" educational approach. By "cookbook" I refer to the procedure in our part of the world to say, "Here are the ingredients; here are the steps to take to put them together for a guaranteed success."

When we Westerners today seek to share the gospel in

the East, therefore, it becomes crucially essential for us to define our objectives. Paul spoke the truth in Galatians 1:8, "Though we, or an angel from heaven, preach any other gospel unto you than that which we have preached unto you, let him be accursed." Here is a truth that is as valid today as when it was originally uttered. We must not indigenize the essence of the gospel. The gospel always remains the same—Christ came into the world to save sinners.

No, the gospel must not be changed. What must be changed is the expression of the gospel. Unchanging essence, indigenized expression. We must indigenize the means by which we communicate the gospel. The gospel has a universal character. Its essence is universal. There is absolutely no one else comparable to Jesus Christ. Moses, Buddha, and Mohammed cannot stand beside Him. Who Jesus is and what He does for men are both genuinely unique. We must invite men, as the Epistle to the Hebrews puts it, to "consider . . . Christ Jesus." But how, given all of the resistance and resentment which we Westerners have earned for ourselves in the Third World, are we to do it?

Unfortunately, there are some groups who, recognizing the delicacy of the situation and lacking a solid commitment to the essence of the gospel, have espoused syncretism. They seek to combine Christianity with other religions. This has been a total failure on all fronts. The demands of Christ are absolute, and there is no way to combine them with any other religion. (Historically, Islam is a strong example of this very thing. Jesus is revered by Muslims as a great prophet, but He is rejected as Lord and Savior. The net results is that Jesus has no effect in the lives of Muslims. Either you accept Jesus as your Lord and Savior, or else you do not actually accept Him at all.)

Meeting People Where They Are

Living in another part of the world does not necessarily mean understanding that part of the world. Just because a plantation owner has worked with black people for many years does not mean that he necessarily understands black people. Just because a Westerner has spent years in business or education or religion in another part of the world does not mean that he necessarily understands that part of the world.

There are two extremes, and both miss the mark. One is aloofness and isolation; the other is a phony togetherness in which a person pretends not to be himself. When I went to Indonesia, a well-meaning and enthusiastic college co-ed suggested that the only way that I would ever enjoy the acceptance of the Indonesians was by living with them in their own houses. She urged me to eat their own food and adopt their other customs. I flatly rejected this, and I can say, with no little evidence to support it, that I have been accepted in Indonesia from one end to the other. I have enjoyed acceptance among all ranks of intellectuality, in all strata of society, and in all echelons of culture. I illustrated my concept to the concerned co-ed in this way.

When I am in Indonesia, I tell my friends there that it is essential that I get my sleep. I'll be glad to put in sixteen or eighteen hours a day in the heat, but I must be in a cool place—cool by their standards—in order to get my sleep. Then I told her that I pointed to one of my friends, John DeFretes, and said, "John, when you came to my house, I turned off my air conditioning. I did this because I knew that you were not accustomed to that kind of temperature and to be subjected to it could bring about sickness. Is that not right?"

"Now, I am in your country, and I am not accustomed to

this heat and humidity. I must turn on the air conditioning, at least during my sleeping hours. Does this make sense?"

"Of course, and we want you to be comfortable."

The point is that there must be an understanding. It's a mood, a nonverbal desire to cooperate and accommodate.

Many people try so hard to win acceptance that their efforts come off as patronizing condescension. This is as naturally resented in the countries of the non-West as it is in the West. Nobody likes a phony.

David Barrett observes that from a historical point of view, leadership of world missions is "rapidly passing from the Western churches to the new and dynamic third-world communities." He says that these communities are unfettered by many of the forces crippling their Western counterparts. The consequences of this for the future influence of Christianity in the world are incalculable.

Ethiopia has rejected the imposition of foreign cultural mores. From the beginning she has maintained complete charge of her own spiritual activities, although she has willingly shared her opportunities with the foreign mission.

It is even wrong for a foreigner to come in and say, "We must build a strong national church." This is inimical to the pattern of Paul the Apostle, and it is greatly resented by local people. The implication is that local people are not adequate to read the Bible, interpret the Scriptures, and respond to the leadership of the Holy Spirit. It is assumed that they must be directed by foreign forces.

In recent years, the words "population explosion" has been on everyone's lips. But what do they mean? Well, the population of the world increases by more than 80 million people a year. Hold on a second; don't let that slip by.

Eighty million people is a third of all the people in the United States! It is ten times the population of New York City.

Every three years, the world adds as many new people as the entire population of the United States.

Let that soak in. The entire population of our country every three years.

Each year, as world population increases by nearly 80 million, world Christianity is increasing by about 7 million. We are winning, year by year, no more than a tenth of the population *increase*. World growth is running away and leaving us behind. Each year, the percentage of the world's peoples who calls itself Christian drops. Face the facts. We are failing to carry the gospel to every creature. Christ's command is plain, but we are not obeying it. What must we do?

There are, after all, only two elements in the proclamation of the gospel—the message and the method. We stand unequivocally for the conviction that the message is right. The inescapable conclusion remaining to us is that the method must be wrong. Surely, Jesus did not commission us to failure.

I have long been of the opinion that there is little of inspiration to be found in the records of failure. It is the clear leading of logic to study the records of success. In all the pages of sacred history, there are few greater achievements than those of the Apostle Paul. In A.D. 47 there were no churches in the areas which were to make up his initial field of service—Galatia, Macedonia, Achaia, and Asia. In A.D. 57—after just ten years of labor—Paul could speak of his work in these regions as finished. There were strong churches in all of the great cities of the region. He trusted the converts to carry the gospel to the surrounding

Maramon Convention, India, one of largest annual convocations of Christians in the world

countryside. He set himself to go westward into new areas of need.

On the premise that there is more to be learned by studying successes than failures, let us look objectively at the method of St. Paul. In contrasting it to the prevalent methods of our own time, we can seek to discover a workable strategy that will replace the failures and stagnation of recent years. This study of Paul's work is the basis for the methods to be set forth in remaining chapters. These methods, in fact, have been proving themselves already during the past five years. God is at work even now. There is hope for planet earth.

Act on Your Hope

1. Pray that Christian leaders of the world may see more clearly the need to present the essence of the gospel without cultural restrictions.

2. Read the New Testament for yourself, looking for statements of the essence of the gospel. Write down key verses as you find them. Prepare a summary statement of what is essential in presenting the gospel to any person.

12

Isolation Competes with Emulation

Paul the Apostle knew where he was going and why. He was a man with clear convictions, binding commitments, fixed goals, and identified priorities. If we are to take an effective part in carrying out Christ's Commission, we must set our house in order just as Paul did.

Paul's basic convictions were that men are lost and cannot save themselves and that Christ is the only Savior. His supreme commitment was to Christ as the one and only Lord of his life—"Christ liveth in me" (Gal. 2:20), "for me to live is Christ" (Phil. 1:21). His highest goal was to share the good news of Christ as widely as possible. His priorities were set to carry out his goal effectively; he gave himself to the things that would make Christ known. He set aside those things—however natural or desirable from a human standpoint—that did not contribute to meeting his goal.

Examine your own life honestly. What are your real convictions and commitments? Do you have definite goals? Do you set priorities and act on them? If so, what are they? Unless Christ is really the Lord of your life, it is unlikely that your goals and priorities resemble those of Paul. If

Christ is your supreme Lord, do you have the goals and priorities that express His lordship effectively?

Paul did not find a comfortable place and settle there. He moved out, under the leadership of the Holy Spirit, to fresh fields—places where needs were greater than those in the areas where he had been. Tarsus was his home, but he didn't stay there. In Antioch, he had friends and supporters, but he did not stay there. Each new city he entered proved to have its own peculiar hazards, but he pressed on, going to the areas of greatest need. He worked in cities such as Ephesus and Corinth long enough to win and train reliable leaders to carry on his work, but he stayed no longer than necessary.

Paul did not let the people around him set his goals and priorities.

We from the West, especially, must learn this from him.

Groping for Meaning

For at least a decade now, America has been in a spiritual quandary. Many are not sure about our purpose as a nation. They are not sure about our relationship to other nations of the world. They are not sure that life really has a purpose. Christians have been infected with this national disease. But we have no reason to be. The man without Christ may very well wonder about purposes, relationships, and meanings. The man in Christ can be certain about all three.

Part of the American debate is over isolation. In recent years, Vietnam has been the focus of whether or not we should become involved in the life of other nations. In fact, of course, the debate should not be over *whether* we should be involved but rather over *how* we should be involved. Involved we must be. We can't escape that, even when we try. The people of the world are out there, pushing against our doors. Isolation has never really been possible, but today it is even less possible than in the past. The transportation facilities of the present demand interaction with others.

The real question is over what our relationship should be—how we interact. Christian faith is very much at the center of the issues we face. War is a prime example. William James pointed out long ago that war is the result of emptiness—spiritual emptiness, if you will see the full picture. Because men suffer emptiness, they conclude that getting additional things—material spoils, the pride that goes with conquest—can fill the void. Aggression is the result, creating in others the desire for defense. War is then the natural consequence.

God, through Christ, can fill the gaps in men's lives. When that happens, war will be a thing of the past.

We cannot afford spiritual isolationism.

As people grope for meaning and purpose, they make some strange choices. It never ceases to amaze me that some who appeal most vociferously for isolation are really given over to emulation. They claim that we should mind our own business, but they devote themselves to copying the beliefs and practices of others.

For example, in many American cities you can see groups of young people with shaved heads and orange robes. They are walking up and down the streets, chanting "Hare Krishna, Hare Krishna." Over and over they chant, "Hare Krishna, Hare Krishna, Hare, Hare, Krishna, Krishna."

These young people follow a cult whose roots are in Hinduism. They do not believe that this is the age of Aquarius but the age of Kali—the age of destruction and hypocrisy. They say this age began 5,000 years ago and is destined to continue until the year 428,970. They keep chanting the name of a god. Are they mental derelicts? No. Many of them have graduate degrees. There are 500 such groups across America.

By contrast to the indifference and self-indulgence of so many American professing Christians, notice some things about them.

The Hare Krishna cultists do not eat meat. They will not take intoxicating drinks. They do not participate in sex outside of a wedded relationship. They scorn gambling. And, in addition to the normal definition of gambling, they include idle words, sports, time wasting of any kind including mental speculation. Contrary to the thrust of women's lib, when a girl marries within the Hare Krishna group, she accepts unquestioning subordination to her husband. These young people are flotsam of urban depersonalization in the United States. They are culture-shocked youth who believe that they have lived life without meaning, and they are searching for meaning.

How tragic an indictment on Christianity! We know the true meaning of life, but we fail to make it evident to those around us. Our own young people are groping around and searching for something overseas that they do not seem able to find at home.

We have known for some time that some famous entertainment personalities, such as the Beatles and Mia Farrow, have journeyed to India to secure help from an Indian guru. The press has even informed us that some of America's leading companies employ the services of Indian mystics to assist them in the practical operations of their businesses—to help them with their personnel. It grieves me that some who call themselves Christians show more interest in the response of a Ouija board than they do in the leadership of the Holy Spirit. As Christians we can have God's leadership. We have no need for leadership from non-Christian sources.

Freedom or Slavery?

If we had been spiritual internationalists years ago, we could afford to be military isolationists today. It is regrettable that we export more pornography than we do Christ-like living.

For example, on one trip I left the airport in Bangkok, Thailand, smarting under some of the American literary garbage that was in the bookstand there. I then flew nonstop to Tashkent, USSR, where I, along with the other passengers on that SAS trans-Asian flight, were herded to the terminal during the refueling of the giant DC-8. There was no pornography in that Russian airport. Rather there was serious literature on dialectical materialism, the philosophy of Marx, Lenin, and other Communist leaders. The material was available in many languages and offered at prices so reasonable that almost anyone could afford it.

The contrast between the literary representation of America in Bangkok and that of the USSR in Tashkent shocked me.

We then flew nonstop to Copenhagen, Denmark. Copenhagen had just concluded its first international pornographic convention. Sodom and Gomorrah would have blushed at the reports of the activities of that convention. I thought of the freedom that we have in the United States and of that enjoyed in Denmark. I reflected on the evangelical background of both nations and asked myself, "Why?" Why did godless atheistic Russia give every outward appearance of having a more defined national purpose than either of these great nations? I then concluded that freedom can be a blessing, but it can be made a curse. We may so misuse freedom as to forge the chains of our own enslavement.

Only to the extent that we exercise discipline do we enjoy freedom. A stone obeys one law, the law of gravity, and it remains motionless. A worm obeys two laws, the laws of gravity and motion. It can remain still on the ground, or it can move. A bird obeys three laws—gravity, motion, and aerodynamics. It can stand still, walk, or fly. As long as the river is within its banks, it can turn great turbines and generate electricity. When the river overflows its banks, it brings death and destruction.

When nations use their liberty for other than worthy and God-glorifying ends, they ultimately sign their own warrant for slavery and death.

Recently overseas, one of the great writers of our day said to me, "You must not use my name, John, but you can quote me as saying that my colleagues in America are writing themselves right out of their own freedom. They have turned a jaundiced interpretation of the first amendment into their own ultimate destruction."

No wonder the suicide rates in our western countries are climbing with such staggering speed.

When information about the thousands of American service men in Vietnam hooked on drugs was first published, I started some checking. Right away I called the military attaché's office of the Republic of Korea Embassy in Washington to find out what kind of a problem the Korean soldiers in Vietnam were having. He told me that not one Korean soldier serving in Vietnam had been on drugs and that there absolutely was no problem. I then checked about the Australian and the New Zealand soldiers there. The story was similar. There was nothing among them like the tragedy that struck our men. Why is this? They were under the same conditions, under the same pressures.

There is wide agreement among qualified students of drug abuse. It issues from mental and emotional problems. Here again is a case of transforming freedom into slavery. There is permissiveness in the West, a revolt against authority without punitive response, and a basic weakening of moral fiber in homes and schools. Do not these conditions account for the fact that young men sent to Vietnam to fight a frustrating war became victims of such a life-destroying problem?

When I was speaking to Mr. Jae Ho Kim, the assistant military attaché of the Korean Embassy in Washington, I asked him how he explained the Korean soldiers' freedom from drug involvement. He mentioned two things. One was the shame that it would bring on the people back home. The other was the desire to get a good education and make a success out of life. These strong motivations kept the problem from developing.

American home life could well emulate the home life in many of the nations of the Third World. God promised certain blessings on homes that are well-ordered. In such homes, the husband is the head. Husbands love their wives, and wives respect their husbands. Fathers do not provoke their children to wrath, and children give respect to their elders. See Ephesians 5:21—6:4 for the Bible's statement of these truths. This Bible view does not exactly jibe with our wide-spread American assumption that homes are supposed to be "democratic." We need to remember that God's Word is our sure source of wisdom. American folkways can be—and sometimes are—fallacious. When the father abrogates his responsibilities to his wife and children, the result is not democracy but anarchy. Children are not blessed by being given "freedom" but are blighted by inadequate parental support, guidance, and discipline.

One of the reasons that the young American Republic flourished was the solidarity of the home.

Mobility, money, and leisure time can produce great blessings or, prostituted, they can be a curse. These factors when controlled with a God-honoring self-discipline can produce great music, write great books, launch great programs, eventuate in great achievements and outstanding blessings for all men.

The Secret of Greatness

It is high time for our nation to export those qualities that made her great. It is high time for us as Christians to accept our responsibilities for calling America to return to Christian values. We are called by God to spiritual warfare, not to be namby-pamby and wishy-washy. We seem to think that we ought to try to please everybody and end up pleasing nobody. This is not what Paul the Apostle was talking about when he said that he was "all things to all men." He put himself in the other fellow's place, but he never failed to stand for the truth.

The nations of the world have their eyes on America. What a responsibility! What an opportunity!

In 1955 the nations of Africa and Asia met in Bandung, Indonesia, for an Afro-Asian conference. The United States did not even send an observer. Washington was convinced that the conference would be Communist-oriented. Furthermore, Sukarno was giving America a bad time. However, the keynote address began, "We convene here on the 179th anniversary of Paul Revere's ride." The speaker identified with America's fight for liberty.

Probably no man of our time has done more for the American image overseas than Dr. Bob Pierce, founder of World Vision. Some time back I was high in the hills of Southern India when I came upon a clearing and saw a great hospital. The inscription on the cornerstone indicated that it had been laid by Dr. Bob Pierce in 1954. I visited an orphanage in Central Java—founded by Dr. Bob Pierce. On the way from the Chosun Hotel in downtown Seoul, Korea, out to the airport you pass the World Vision headquarters, situated majestically on a hill. It gives mute testimony to an American missionary-evangelist whose prayer was, "Let my heart be broken with the things that break the heart of God."

Dr. Christie Wilson, who has served the people of Afghanistan so nobly since the late forties, told me of flying with Bob Pierce from Kabul, Afghanistan, to Russia. The plane set down in Tehran, Iran, for refueling. While the men were in the airport, they overheard the news of the earthquake south of Tehran. With characteristic swiftness of assessment followed by decisive action, Pierce said to Wilson, "We've got to help these people." In a matter of hours, he had secured the use of a private plane, enlisted the help of a pilot, secured the specialized ministry of a nurse, and acquired all available medicines. Repeatedly in the little plane packed with supplies, Pierce—at great personal hazard—brought healing and for many stayed the hand of imminent death.

This man started walking the world—alone—back in the late forties. Over the intervening years he has established orphanages, missions, hospitals, leprosariums, sanitariums. He has sponsored pastors' conferences and Bible schools.

A few years ago, when Marshall Green was Ambassador to Indonesia, he told me of his first-hand knowledge of the help Bob Pierce had provided in cementing good relations between the Republic of Korea and the United States.

I personally believe that if a motion picture could be made of the ministry and exploits of this man under God, the young people of our nation and of the world would sit in wide-eyed amazement. I believe God would use it to challenge them to lives of purpose and meaning they never dreamed possible.

There is a choice before America, but the choice is also before you as an individual Christian. What are your commitments? What are your priorities? Are you contributing to the hope for planet earth?

Act on Your Hope

1. Learn about agencies that are engaged in Bible distribution around the world. Find out about the work of such groups as the American Bible Society, the Gideons, and the Wycliffe Bible Translators. Find your place in the support of such organizations through prayer, financial contributions, and other ways. Do your part to be sure that America exports the Word of God and not merely trash or pornography.

2. Learn what your community is doing to stop the flow of obscene materials. Call your district attorney or police chief for information. Find out and act on what you should do as a private citizen.

13

Evangelize Now

Paul trained local Christians to win their areas as he moved on to other fields.

Jesus started with individuals. Christianity became a world-wide movement through simple fishermen like Peter, gray-flanneled tax collectors like Matthew, and idealistic youths like John.

Evangelism International has taken the methods of Jesus and Paul—and applied them through the expanded means of communication of our time. We call this strategy "Total Evangelism—Plus." This program has now been in operation for five years. Its results can be seen around the world today.

Five Steps to Win

The strategy of "Total Evangelism—Plus" is based on a five-step program that begins and ends with the individual. The program is designed for citywide or nationwide projects, some results of which have been reported in earlier pages of this book. God has blessed the approach in nations in various parts of the world—all the way from the Far East to Portugal. The reliance on local personnel means that the quality of each nation's culture and way of life is adequately incorporated into the work there. The gospel is never compromised or watered-down, but each nation hears it in ways suited to its own characteristics.

Step 1: training the lay witnesses.—Jesus trained 70 disciples and sent them out. Evangelism International strategy is to send out fully equipped, modern-day disciples to witness in churches, schools, clubs, and so forth. The training of these national Christians is a key part of the program. A two-week (five hours a day) session is provided for this purpose. This training is directed by a qualified third-world Christian leader or be a Western leader who understands the non-West, nonwhite mind and who is accepted by the nationals. We thus start with individual Christians.

Step 2: simultaneous evangelism.—Depending on the scope of the target area, the trained witnesses spread throughout the nation or city, witnessing and counseling in participant churches. In some areas such as Indonesia and Korea, crusades have been nationwide in scope. The two crusades in Portugal in 1970 and 1972 concentrated on two large urban areas, Lisbon and Oporto.

The focus of step two is simultaneous crusades throughout the target area. Participating churches have lay witnesses and guest preachers, usually for 10 days. The same guest preacher stays in a church for the entire period. Visiting laymen move from one church to another. A visiting preacher works in a church of his own denomination. This program crosses denominational lines by gaining participation of all churches in an area who will join. In Indonesia, for example, the two largest groups were the Presbyterians and the Pentecostals. For the first time ever, they cooperated—in a Total Evangelism—Plus campaign.

Step 3: united crusade evangelism.—Following the careful preparation laid in steps one and two, we have a mass crusade, uniting all the ingredients of the previous steps. These mass meetings are conducted at the invitation and under the sponsorship of local Christian leaders. They have been unusually fruitful in communicating the gospel. Decisions for Christ, as recorded by local sponsors, have repeatedly numbered in the thousands.

Step 4: local seminar on evangelism.—The last two phases of Total Evangelism—Plus are devoted to a ministry of follow-up. This is designed to insure the strengthening of the Christian witness in the population-exploding lands into which Evangelism International enjoys unique entree. Step four is a "floating seminar" for local Christian leaders. The subject is biblical principles of total evangelization. This step is a sequel to the training of lay witnesses in step one. It seeks to produce a leadership climate in which evangelism will be an on-going function of the churches.

Step 5: international training program.—The ultimate phase of Evangelism International's program is designed to implement the Great Commission in areas closed or closing to Western personnel. The concept behind this part of the program was introduced in Chapter 1 and will be further developed in the remaining part of the present chapter. This program is restricted to carefully selected key Christian leaders from Third World nations. It brings them to Singapore to study together under the leadership of third-world authorities on evangelization. Men are selected who will return to their homes and train others to join them in the work for which they have been prepared.

A Look at Haggai Institute

A group of twenty to twenty-five men come to Singapore for 200 hours of intensive training in effective Christian evangelization and witnessing. The ninth session, concluded April 4, 1973, brought the total of alumni to 181. These are men who occupy leadership roles in their own nations comparable to those of Norman Vincent Peale and Bishop Fulton Sheen in America.

These men who have met in Singapore often have come from great distances—not only from the Far East but from such other Third World areas as Africa, the Mideast, and Latin America. All have come at personal sacrifice. Evangelism International pays a large share of their expenses, but each helps to pay part of his own—at what frequently amounts to a sizeable part of his total annual income. At the last session, there was one man who walked 32 miles to begin his journey. There was the chaplain of a huge Korean university. An Indonesian working on a master's degree in electrical engineering was in attendance. An Ethiopian Eastern Orthodox priest sat across the table from a clergy leader of South India.

The faculty for this session—as for those before it—read like a Who's Who of Third-World evangelical leaders. Among them was Dr. Kyung Chik Han, founder and long-time pastor of the great Young Nak Presbyterian Church of Seoul, Korea. This church of 16,000 members is the world's largest in the Presbyterian fellowship. Dr. Timothy Yu, from Hong Kong, is a Christian communications expert. Dr. Chandu Ray, now an evangelical leader in Singapore, formerly was Anglican Bishop of Karachi, Pakistan. He is one of the world's great Christian preachers. Rev. James Wong is one of Asia's leading authorities on church growth and the founder of a worldwide prayer movement. Monsieur Jean Andre is a European businessman who has reached more than 50,000 youngsters with the gospel of

Christ. Dr. G. D. James is a an evangelist from Singapore whose work has reached throughout Southeast Asia. Dr. Petrus Octavianus is a specialist in Christian outreach from Indonesia.

The men in atendance are diverse in age and position. Many are mature and highly educated. Some are younger, but all are at least 25 years old. All have proven themselves as Christian leaders in their own areas. A striking case of an unusually young man who already has won himself a leadership position is that of Rev. Kongoe Sipwanji (pronounced *Kongoy Swangee*). His trip to Singapore to attend the training session was his first away from his home area, the western highlands of New Guinea. Converted in 1963, he has been preaching almost ever since. At the time of his trip to Singapore, he was acting as principal of a Baptist training school.

Sipwanji reported afterwards that his training has contributed to the development of the curriculum in his school. His notes from the seminar have been used in teaching Christian leadership. He wrote, "I am translating the notes from English to the Kyaka language. My 23 students are very interested in studying about the leadership work."

The training seminars in Singapore were early identified by the name of Evangelism International, the sponsoring agency. As they have developed into a major and very specialized function of the parent body, the need was recognized for a specific designation. The board of Evangelism International has thus named this program Haggai Institute. I do not take this as a personal recognition so much as a recognition of the vital and continuing nature of the work—and the name is a third-world name. Thanks to God for all of the evidence that we have launched an approach that is making a difference for Christ in so many areas.

At the human level, our reliance is heavy on the great Christians of the Third World who conduct almost all of the seminars. I see my own role as largely catalytic. In view of the caliber of participants, we also rely on them for much of the input. We learn together; we learn from each other.

"One of the greatest things about these seminars is that they bring together Christians from all over the world. Divisive forces are minimized, suspicion is broken down." This opinion from one who attended the spring session of 1973 captures a real part of the overall intention. The same alumnus added, "The Institute establishes the common denominator Christians of all cultures have in Christ, as well as the authority of the Scripture and the mandate to carry out the Great Commission."

The Institute program is based on a clear commitment to the gospel and the meeting of specific needs that usual Christian training largely overlooks. We do not compete with seminaries and Bible schools in the scope of academic subjects. Rather we concentrate on basics of evangelization.

First, in order that our doctrinal commitments ever be before us, we have a doctrinal overview. The Bibles serves as the sole basis of our doctrine. We deal with the sovereignty of God and the Great Commission—God's right to command and our need to obey. We survey the gospel—its meaning, its power, its adequacy, and the believer's response and responsibility. We look at the priorities of the gospel—what may be called the essential elements. Along with the importance of evangelism, we consider the person and work of God the Father, the Lord Jesus Christ, and the Holy Spirit. We study salvation as taught in the Scriptures, including the relationship of law and grace.

This doctrinal overview particularly stresses the application of Christ's redemption. Specific applications include faith, repentance, regeneration, and related subjects. Also included are sanctification, assurance, and prayer. The approach to such topics is biblical. Western trappings are avoided. Searching questions are raised which participants answer from their own knowledge and experience. The result is twofold—compelling Christian certainties are brought into sharper focus and participants aid and stimulate each other. The result is cross-pollenization. The *implications* of the gospel are brought out—the actions that Christians should take in response to the truth that they know.

As a result, seminar members see new applications that are appropriate for their particular situations. For example, the testimony of Koreans proclaiming the gospel in North Korea despite Communist domination there, has caused Latin Americans to see new ways for witnessing in the face of local Communism.

Additional Study Areas

The doctrinal overview is basic to everything else, but most of the Haggai Institute curriculum is devoted to training in skills—ways that Christians can go to work. People who are invited to take part are already committed Christians. They come in order to learn better ways of making their Christian testimony effective.

Hence the area of communications is given strong attention. Here is an area where the secular world has forged ahead, even though we Christians have the world's most vital message to communicate. The Institute seeks to redress this imbalance by sharing with participants the best current knowledge of how to get a message across all of the barriers that keep one person from hearing and responding to another.

Youth have always been of crucial significance in effective Christian life. Undoubtedly, some of Jesus' first disciples were young. Our hope for revival in America appears to lie with the young. True revival can come only through the leadership and empowering of the Holy Spirit, but somehow the young seem especially suited to hearing what the Spirit would tell us. We thus have a major study area devoted to youth—getting through to them, winning them, mobilizing them for Christ, and using their assets in the total program of Christian outreach.

Another area where the secular world has broken ground that Christians need to occupy is the development of personal resources. Goals are critical for secular success. How should Christians apply the goal setting process? This is explored in depth, along with such areas as discipline and imagination. We examine the relationship of self-discipline and Spirit-discipline. We see the role of imagination in human behavior—a factor much stronger, if you please, than will.

Related topics in the development of personal resources include the art of "picturization," the value of an affirmative mental attitude and of a God-glorifying self-image. Hence the insights of secular psychology are brought directly to bear on vital Christian living. Ironically, the Bible gives ample testimony to such practical matters. The secular world, however, has capitalized on them more clearly than the Christian world has to date. This is contrary to the counsel of Christ, who urged us to employ practical wisdom when we are about His business. See Matthew

10:16 and Luke 16:8. We are to rely on the Spirit, but we are also to do our best.

Another major curriculum area is methods of evangelism. Eight different approaches to evangelism are considered, starting with the basics—personal and church. Evangelistic outreach must have its foundation here, but the demand of the present is that other methods also be used. Hence we consider such areas as industry and business, exploring methods that are suited to circumstances in those fields of activity.

The Christian witness in the non-Christian culture is a vital subject for study. On the one hand, we consider the blight of syncretism—the fact that Christ cannot be blended with other religions. On the other, we study the nature and necessity for Christian unity. Recall what has been said in previous chapters about the difference between unity and union. The program at Haggai Institute, just as the mass crusades of Evangelism Internation, brings together Christians from across denominational lines. Not only Protestants but those of various Catholic traditions are included. This is true of seminar leaders as well as participants. The result is not an effort to achieve structural union or even uniformity in viewpoint. We see, rather, the blessed unity in the Spirit, in which men of differing traditions work together for our crucial purposes as servants of our one Lord, Jesus Christ.

This area of witness in non-Christian cultures is expanded by studying results from work in such diverse areas as Indonesia, the Arab world, and Africa. It includes an in-depth study of Paul's ministry at Athens.

At Athens, Paul proclaimed the full-orbed gospel—the nature of God, the centrality of Christ, and the reality of human need. He corrected the insidious errors that still blight men, all the way from atheism's claim that God doesn't exist to universalism's false optimism that everyone will eventually be saved.

Finally, the Haggai Institute curriculum focuses attention on the laws of leadership. Have you ever stopped to think how critical leadership is in the work of God? Consider how largely the Bible is a book about leaders—Abraham, Moses, Elijah, and Isaiah, to name only four from the Old Testament. Remember how Jesus found his leaders in unlikely places—the varied backgrounds of the first disciples and the stubborn recalcitrance of Saul of Tarsus before his conversion. God is in the business of recruiting leaders. We seek to work under the leadership of His Spirit to help men He has enlisted unfold their gifts. We see how good leaders are willing to learn from their mistakes. We note Bible insights as well as secular wisdom from business and other everyday activities. This area is practical and detailed, going into illustrations of how leadership works.

As part of teaching leadership, we teach how the seminar can be reproduced. We can never bring all of the men to Singapore who need the type of training that we offer. Instead, we train the top leadership. They go back to their nations and train other leaders. One of the early fruits of this work has already been reported in an earlier chapter. The area of Assam is located in northeast India, near China. White "preaching" missionaries have been expelled. Three alumni of one of our early sessions, however, have gone to Assam and trained 193 local Christians on the basis of the program outlined above. As a result, Christian outreach in Assam has been gloriously strengthened according to national leaders there.

Here, then, is the proverbial "bird's eye view" of a work

whose depth and stimulation cannot possibly be put on paper. Imagine sitting in a room with twenty-five of the world's keenest, most dedicated Christians—men of widely varied backgrounds and nationalities. Picture the excitement and stimulation as these men share insights and experiences. Think of the thrill that comes to them as their faith is broadened and deepened by learning that the Christ who is so real to them is equally real to men from the other side of the earth. Note the courage and strength they gain from each other as they share experiences of victory in the power of the Holy Spirit.

And with all of this is the practical sharing of truths and methods that many have no other means of learning about. Indeed, some of these methods are foreign to the West. So much of what is taught at Haggai Institute can come only as one life touches another directly. We are dealing with realities that need to be seen in action. Furthermore, we are making applications of knowledge and skill from the intellectual and business communities Christians have not made before. All of this is done within the clear framework of evangelical commitments and priorities. All is done to the glory of God and the winning of men to Christ.

What Is Your Part?

Evangelism International and the Haggai Institute depend on the prayers and financing of God's people. We stress personal, local support and participation in all of our work. All of our crusades are carried out with local planning, local personnel, and local financing in so far as possible. Every man who comes to Singapore to attend the Institute pays a share of his expenses. This is not a charity program seeking merely to funnel American dollars to overseas people. By calling for this kind of involvement

Seminar in North India

from all of those with whom we work, we do more than profit from their wisdom and their knowledge of their own people. We also gain a level of participation that no imported program can ever win.

Yet the work requires support from America and other nations. Christians in Switzerland gave over $37,000 in 1972. Several thousand dollars came from Asia. The cost of bringing a man to Singapore is between $2,500 and $3,600. With the present trend in costs, it undoubtedly will shortly be more. National Christians from the third world do not have that kind of money. Without strong continuing support, the program cannot be maintained. The real challenge, of course, it not merely to maintain it but to expand it.

Vale Formosa Theater, Oporto, Portugal—Crowd waiting for seats during Crusade

This program is not a substitute for traditional missions. It is a supplement. It reaches into areas where traditional missionaries are restricted or excluded. It develops a kind of involvement by national Christians that traditional missions cannot secure.

The face of world Christianity is in transition. Throughout much of the third world, most Christian growth is among Pentecostals. In Africa, in one nation after another, large groups of national Christians are withdrawing from denominations that are supported by overseas mission boards and forming new church bodies under African leadership. In both cases, we see the fact that national Christians are taking their spiritual destinies into their own hands. For Pentecostalism, like the African national churches, is essentially an indigenous movement.

Evangelism International and the Haggai Institute are not contributing to break-away movements and sentiments. Instead, we are seeking to prepare and involve a quality of Third World Christian leadership that will have the same virtues and appeals as the breakaway groups. We can no longer win the world by old-fashioned, Western paternalism. We cannot remake the world's peoples into our Western image, in spite of how dear it is to us. We must regain the insights of Jesus and of Paul, who understood and accepted people individually.

We must enable national Christians to fulfill the roles that volume of prayer that went up from America when it appeared that the Astronauts of Apollo 13 might not get back to earth safely. As worthy as that concern was, how much more worthy is the concern of Christian people for carrying out Christ's Commission. We have the world's best news, the answer to men's deepest needs. But our present level of proclamation is not adequate to tell the world of Jesus Christ. Traditional missions cannot go to Burma, North Korea, China, or many other areas of the world. We must have ways that rely on national Christians. We must enable national Christians to fulfill the roles that only they can.

Dr. Donald E. Hoke is founder and former president of Japan Christian College and now director of the 1974 International Congress on Evangelism in Lausanne, Switzerland. He has pointed out the following values in the program of Haggai Institute:

1. The exposure of younger national leaders to a broad fellowship of the Church of Christ in both an international and an interdenominational dimension.

2. Acquainting these men with various personalities, types of work, emphases, etc.

3. Deepening the sense of love and loyalty toward the true Church of Jesus Christ which is superdenominational, supernational, and superracial.

4. The strong desire of Evangelism International leaders to help the national church.

5. The ability of Evangelism International to increase the interest in missions among people in North America by means of promoting this.

Here, then, are some insights of an observer whose own work is quite distinct from that of Evangelism International.

The most encouraging exaluation comes from the letters of the men who have returned to their homes from Singapore. Evangelism International publishes a newsmagazine, *Straight from the Shoulder,* which has published dozens of these through recent years. There are more, of course, than space in the magazine permits us to publish. The letters report gratitude, encouragement, and victory. Here are excerpts from two that have been received recently.

The first comes from Kerala, in the southern part of India. The writer is K. J. Matthew. He says, "I have returned from Singapore, after participating in the Evangelism International. Truly, I was blessed very much being a participant in it. I am putting into practice, all what I have learned there. From the very next day of my arrival I am engaged in the business of the Lord. I am training men to be soul winners. We are seeing good success in it. Almost on every day I have to preach in meetings. They are not very big meetings, but, the number is increasing day by day. I take time to prepare messages and preach. And therefore, people are overanxious to hear the message."

Another writer is K. P. Yohannan, who lives in New

Businessmen's Banquet, Oporto, Portugal

Delhi. He says, "Already I have begun to share the EI siminar message with my friends and they are really excited over this.

"Doctor, with all my heart I can say that this EI seminar has been the greatest blessing in my life outside of my salvation. I believe God has a great ministry for me in the days to come.

"I continue to pray that the Lord will use EI for the blessing of those in Asia."

Such excerpts give only a hint of what the writers are experiencing. God is blessing those who attend the Institute, and through them he is blessing others.

The thrust of the Institute's training is outreach. Those who are trained are committed toward training others. Here is the strategy of Jesus and of Paul in action. Jesus said, "Go into all the world." Through the crusades of

Evangelism International we are going into much of the world, but there are areas where we cannot go in person. In neutral Singapore, however, we are meeting with men from such areas. We are going into their homelands through them. The Haggai Institute is a unique way by which we go into areas that are closed to all of the traditional ways. Its alumni are not only trained to witness but also to train those who are won as witnesses. Here, indeed, is a practical strategy for going into all the world.

Proven results are demonstrated in the work of early trainees. Samuel G. O. Sarandatu of Sarabaja, Indonesia, is one of these. He attended the very first training session. Here is a recent report of his work; it is dated September 19, 1972: "From July 15 to August 15, cooperating with MV Logos in North Sulawesi, [we conducted] a Pastor's conference attended by 560 persons for four days; a three day Youth Conference on board ship with 125 in attendance; a Christian Business Men's Conference, attended by 50; and then, as a climax, we conducted a four-evening International Rally, which was attended by approximately 15,000. Meanwhile, our [crusade] team preached in churches.

"Similar activities took place in Ambon, Menado and Kupang.

"During the Surabaja crusade, an average of 1,000 came forward each night at the time of the invitation. The most glorious scene was the last night when almost half of the audience came forward, probably 3,000!

"In April or May of 1973, we hope to have as many key Christian leaders in East Indonesia as possible for a ten-day training seminar, and ten days of open-air evangelistic preaching.

"May God bless you abundantly as you serve Him."

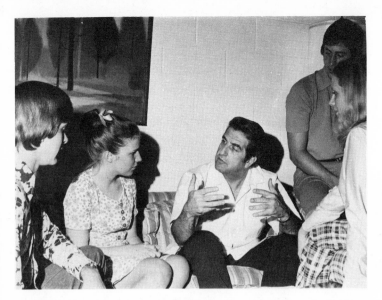

Dr. Haggai talks to students at Baptist College, Charleston, South Carolina

Jesus said, "By their fruits ye shall know them." The fruit of the training program can now be seen around the world.

Act on Your Hope

1. Pray for the work of Evangelism International and Haggai Institute. Search for the support that is appropriate for you under God's leadership—financial contributions, informing your pastor and other church leaders, requesting that the film "Door to Peace" be shown in your church (available from Evangelism International, Box 13, Atlanta, Georgia 30301), and other ways.

2. Seek the involvement of your friends in this work by telling them about it, sharing this book, praying that God will guide them in finding their place of support.

Epilogue

One of the most significant steps in the development of E.I.'s world evangelism training program was consummated recently in Singapore with the official incorporation of Evangelism International as a public company under the laws of the Republic of Singapore.

The final documents were executed after several weeks of negotiations. The documents state that "Evangelism International Incorporated Limited" is organized (among other purposes):

"To establish and carry on in Singapore and or elsewhere an institute, college, school or centre where Christian leaders may obtain on moderate terms a sound religious and general leadership training of the highest order."

A most important meaning of the act of incorporation is that Evangelism International and Haggai Institute are not considered as "foreign" operations, but now are clearly a part of Southeast Asia.

It is one of the highest honors which has come to us—to be fully incorporated in the Republic of Singapore. It seemed to me that the moment the papers were signed, there was a different feeling about everything we said and did. We had received a warm welcome in Singapore from leaders of Church and State from the first day, but now I think there is a widespread feeling that E.I. and the Institute are truly co-laborers with our friends in Singapore. We'll see growing evidence of this in the days ahead, I am certain.